Contents

To Everything
A Purpose

by

CHRISTINA MACLEAN

AMBASSADOR

To Everything A Purpose
© Copyright 1994 Christina Maclean

ISBN 1 898787 17 4

Published by
AMBASSADOR PRODUCTIONS LTD
Providence House,
16 Hillview Avenue,
Belfast, BT5 6JR

Preface

That this book has been written is a marvel, that it is going out without editing is an even greater marvel.

For about seven years I have been encouraged and coerced, in turn, by well meaning friends, some now in Glory, to write of my experience with cancer. I flatly refused. The fact that this account now goes out in print is entirely due to the efforts of my friend Elizabeth Keddie who impressed upon an author friend her conviction that I should take up my pen. As a consequence I was approached and invited to place 'my story', as it was called, on record.

It was a hard decision. The rightness of it was not immediately apparent and some two to three months elapsed before I finally accepted that the Lord purposed.

The book is by no means scholarly. It is a simple account of a journey through life from birth and involves other persons, family or friends, whom I have had the privilege of meeting, or being part of, during this journey. It goes out with one aim, the desire that by God's blessing readers will be comforted and reassured and God glorified.

I would like to express my gratitude to all who encouraged and helped me in any way; including the publishers, whose decision it was to produce this book without any changes.

The proceeds from the sale of the book are to be donated to Cancer Relief Macmillan Fund and the Marie Curie Foundation.

Christina Maclean

Foreword

Only a passing mention can be made of some of the interesting qualities of this book. To say that it is distinctly autobiographical is superfluous.

In its wide-ranging coverage of changing experiences, the author leads us through childhood days in war-time Glasgow and then into the mainly outdoor existence in the bracing Hebridean air, of a little girl whose expatriate Lewis parents have decided to return home. The interest of this is intensified deeply for fellow Islesmen by the recollection of facets of life now almost forgotten.

The writer has a clear and definite purpose in this book. It is aimed at a certain section of the reading public; those who are afflicted with terminal illness and their families and friends. Undergirding the text is the sort of personal background that authenticates the thinking and the purpose in view. It is a worthwhile achievement in itself. But as the story unfolds it proves to be but a part of what is a much larger whole. The labour of writing was undertaken while the author was supervising the opening of a new nursing home and hospice.

The influence of her Christian faith pervades this production. This makes it truly worthy of its place in literature whose aim is to enrich the lives of hospice patients.

We meet with a Christian's responses to affliction, to bereavement and to the prospect of approaching death. There are case histories of absorbing interest as well as liberal quotations which bring out vividly the courage and hope many Christians have expressed when facing death. We discover examples of the mysterious leadings of divine providence, along life's path.

It is a common enough view, surely, that no one should forego pain relief if such is available. Many would put any qualification of this down to mere foolish bravado. Here we meet with a very positive objection to the administration of drugs simply because it is assumed as an essential; the patient ought to exercise a choice in these decisions.

Some might remind us that four hundred years before Christ, Euripides wrote 'Do not consider painful what is good for you'. And that a century before Aeschylus wrote 'There is advantage in the wisdom won from pain'. The fortitude of Christians in the face of pain and death springs from their acquaintance with the Great Conqueror of Death and Grave!

Rev. A.M. Macleod
Free Church Manse
Kinloch
Isle of Lewis

8th June 1994

chapter one

Sharing

'Doubt knocked at the door Faith answered There was nobody there'.

"**P**lace the earphones over your ears" the presenter suggested, "and you will hear what is said when we are linked to the mainland contributors". Mutely obeying, it came as a surprise and no small relief to discover that the local Gaelic broadcast which dominated the studio was shut out. Perhaps I could now recollect my thoughts. Not so. The microphone, placed strategically in front of each contributor, faced me with menacing erectness, arousing within me a sensitivity about my forthcoming performance. Was this pride or simply nervousness?

Centrally situated on the table around which we were gathered was a large bulb. This flashed green when the presenter started talking and red when the mike was open. "Two minutes to go", the presenter announced. I glanced round the studio; newly constructed, I had not been here before. It was large, airy and comfortably furnished. I could almost forget my mission.

My thoughts flash back over many years: I am a small girl on a visit to my aunt's house. Situated on a shelf, well out of reach, is a brown polished wooden box. I am absolutely fascinated. My aunt turns the knob and a disembodied voice speaks. How can a voice come through that box? It all seemed so unnatural.

The transmission of sound by means of a wireless set was new to our village. We didn't have one in our house, we couldn't afford it, but in any case, my mother was not convinced of the wisdom of owning one. Nonetheless I felt quite proud that my enlightened younger aunt had one, even if I was to hear many times over, "keep quiet till we hear the news".

Cumbersome in many ways, the wireless was our first link with the wider world. True there were the newspapers, but news on the wireless was instantly new. Electricity was not yet a reality in the rural villages and the wireless operated by battery, not a small simple H.T. battery which could be purchased in Woolworths, but a large L.T. battery which had to be kept well charged and the level of acid maintained by the addition of distilled water. An aerial and earth system was a must and the terminals of the accumulator had to be smeared with vaseline to prevent corrosion. What a feat just to hear world news programmes! Little did I then think, or indeed those around me, that one day my voice would project from a similar if more sophisticated instrument. The very suggestion would have seemed as a fable. My thoughts return to the present and I ponder on the providence God has planned for my life, a providence which resulted in a visit to the studio on this wet morning. Truly, 'His thoughts are past finding out'.

Participating in radio broadcasts always disturbs my calm. "Take Murdo", I had said to the presenter when he 'phoned me, "his Gaelic is every bit as good as mine, or better". "Murdo cannot do this", is the response. Intrigued, I listen, for I had thought his request must be for someone to talk about the recent sale of work and auction in aid of the hospice. "We have outlined", he goes on, "a programme which we hope will encourage the development of healthy attitudes towards cancer by enabling the community, and particularly sufferers, to talk more freely about it". I waited with abated breath, I knew what was coming. "We require one more person to share in the programme. I am aware of your own open-ness towards your condition and that, together with your involvement in the hospice, makes you our choice". What could I say? Past experience had taught me that complying was much easier than resistance, as far as this presenter was concerned. However cogent my argument he always set my excuses aside.

Without further ado, he went on to inform me of the composition of the panel. It comprised two persons who had cancer, a doctor employed in a mainland hospice who practiced alternative as well as traditional medicine, two Macmillan Sisters, one of whom was based locally, and any contributor who may wish to 'phone-in'. The programme, in Gaelic, was going out live and was to be the first in a series. I digested this information and haltingly agreed to be involved.

Suddenly I am aroused from my reverie. There is an atmosphere of anticipation. Is it fear, is it excitement? I take a sip of water. The presenter is giving the operator a hand signal, the nine second signature tune begins to play, the operator opens the faders, the green light flashes, followed by the red, the microphones are open, we are on the air! A few rapid heart beats increase the adrenalin level, I hear the presenter address the first question to my studio companion, "when you were told you had cancer, were you given enough information and were you advised of the support available?" "No" is the ready response. "I was told very little but when I became acquainted with 'Cul Taic', the cancer support group, I found this enormously helpful". "What were your reactions when you were first told?" the presenter pursues. "I went out and made my will and told my family," is the forthright reply.

The presenter turns to face me, careful, as he does, to keep his mike close to his lips. He asks, "Can you recollect your reaction when you were first informed?". "Very well", I respond, "although fourteen years have elapsed since my first episode. My general practitioner together with the local consultant surgeon called on me in my home to advise me of the result of my biopsy". "And what were your thoughts at the time", he prompts. "As I saw these doctors off the premises I thought ...cancer...me...death. It was as if I was approaching the great rock Death and it concerned me what lay beyond. In good health we seldom think of death, but this news was stark reality. Where did I stand? Where was I to spend Eternity?" As a quick afterthought I added, "At that time I had been a communicant member of the church for over twenty years".

As the interview continues, the doctor on telephone standby is addressed. She elaborates on her work with cancer patients in the hospice where she is employed and of her success with drug regimes, some of which are homeopathic remedies. She speaks of success and cure rates. I feel concerned that her examples may incite hope where expected cure may only be remission, but I have no opportunity to respond.

The Macmillan Sisters are now questioned about their work with both patients and carers. They give a resume of their involvement, which for one sister includes work with patients receiving radio-therapy and chemotherapy. She emphasises that there is no pain associated with the treatment of radiotherapy. At this point the presenter interrupts; there is an incoming call. He enquires of the gentleman as to his name and engages him in conversation regarding his condition and the average person's reaction to the knowledge of his cancer. The man is very open. He has just returned from hospital having received radiotherapy and outlines the visible region of his cancer. He is aware it provokes reaction in those he meets and feels some would prefer to avoid him. He understands their reaction and is not affected by it. He tries to encourage listeners to the programme, who have or may yet have cancer. "It is not the dread disease it once was", he says, adding, "much can be done for cancer today". He sounds confident and positive as he rings off.

The presenter's next question is addressed to my companion. She makes it known that she has not received radiotherapy or chemo-therapy. Turning to me, I respond by agreeing with previous contribu-tors that pain is not a by-product of radiotherapy, but at the same time the experience is not without feelings. These are often difficult to enumerate.

"Time for one final question", the presenter says as he looks across at me. "You are in the unique position of having cancer and of working in a hospice. Do you find that having cancer helps you in your work?" I am unable to say that it definitely does. I never think that as a consequence I have something special or something additional to bring to bear upon my work. Coping mechanisms are so different, there are no norms and I would never wish to discourage a patient by recounting my own experiences. I only discuss it with patients who, knowing I have cancer, raise it with me. I agreed, I may have relieved anxiety in one patient who, following a bone scan, was very confused over the term 'hot spots'. This incident, I reflected, had brought home to me how we professionals take it almost for granted that the average patient understands our terminology. It is not easy for every patient to question his or her doctor or medical physicist as to confusing results, in any case patients often feel that they are deterring doctors from their work when they ply them with questions. Professionals are, however, only too willing to assist their patients to an understanding of their condition and perhaps this is something which should be put across to the public.

Anxious that I would not leave the programme without glorifying God for His great and infinite goodness, I quickly remarked on how His Presence was so evident to me throughout my disease. In each episode, He was there. I tried briefly to outline how by His Grace my cancer came to be so precious to me that I would never choose to be without it, or choose the knowledge that I had never had it. The broadcast ended.

As I left the studio, having said goodbye to the companion I had so momentarily met for the first time, I pondered over the forty minute programme and reflected on what it may or may not have achieved. Was any listener encouraged or discouraged? Did anyone wish further information? How was it received? I paused in my thoughts. From all Eternity God ordained this broadcast. What a privilege but what a responsibility to be part of it! My contribution is what I am accountable for. Was my Lord glorified? My cancer is nothing, my Lord in it everything. Did this come across?

chapter two

To Everything a Purpose

'God's jewels are often set in tears'.

It is 1936, the year in which it is said human love overcame duty to the Crown. King Edward VIII has been proclaimed King on the death of his father King George V, only to stun the nation with the news of his abdication. The same year, the superliner Queen Mary left on her maiden voyage to New York. A remarkable vessel, she excited admiration through her beauty and was regarded with great affection by those who lovingly built and fitted her. Both these events were regarded by the media as eminently newsworthy.

There were many other significant events in 1936, but the one to which we are to give our attention could not excite the media. Yet, it was an event recorded in the annals of Eternity before the world was.

It is pre-war Glasgow and up in a fourth floor tenement flat a young wife busies herself as she makes the final preparations for her forthcoming confinement. Much 'elbow grease' leaves brasses shining and furniture well polished. The big black range has had a good coat of black-lead and the steel-finishes gleam from the effects of steel wool. The sewing machine and knitting needles have been much in use in recent weeks and the baby's clothes are lovingly laid out in readiness. The husband has been instructed to keep the fire burning and the kettles and pots of water boiling. Towels and draw sheets drape across the brass airing line which runs from side to side of the wooden mantlepiece. Old newspapers which have been collected to cover the floor are piled up at the end of the fender. Has she forgotten anything?, she queries with herself.

Deciding a cup of tea a welcome interlude while awaiting her husband, she crosses the room to the sink in the corner beneath the window. Glancing out she views the street-scene below. Youngsters play happily on the pavement, sometimes spilling out on to the street, their merry laughter resounding through the building. Traffic is minimal; the street is a dead end and few residents own cars. It is a safe area in which to play. Her thoughts turn to the future. Will, one day, her own child's voice mingle with those below?

A glance towards the end of the street reveals a fairly high wall beyond which a shipyard lies. The masts of ships and the tips of cranes are clearly visible over the top, while noise levels are by now companionable in their constant regularity. Two years she has lived here. Two happy years! She reflects on the providence which led them to rent this flat, seeing, as always, the Hand of God in it. There are only two rooms and a central porch which houses the coal bunker. The toilet on the landing is shared with two other families, each having their own key, but this has not presented problems. She returns with her cup of tea to the cosy fireside. This is the house where together she and her husband enjoy the Christian fellowship of their friends and where soon she will bring their first born into the world. She has not worked since she married - to do so was unheard of - and she now looks forward to the additional activity which will fill her day.

The pangs of childbirth herald the awaited event. The midwife has been called and the husband is hovering in the background uncertain as to his role. He has taken time off from his work to be with his wife; he glances at the clock on the mantle shelf; the morning is creeping on so slowly; he hopes it will soon be over. The midwife comes into the room. Something must surely be wrong; he has been asked to call the doctor. Down four flights of stairs he races and into the herbalist's shop. Can he use the telephone?, a scarce commodity in these days!

Returning home, he feels so powerless. In his concern, love points the way. He abandons himself to prayer. Whatever could he do without the Lord to turn to in moments such as these? Yet, he has never openly professed his Lord. It has always seemed such a profound and weighty step; the thought of his own unworthiness has bound him with legalistic cords. But still he prays, still he believes and still he hopes. In this crisis prayer has been as natural to him as breathing. Time and time again he commits his young wife to the Grace of God. He views these moments as among the most anxious in his life. What a blessing the Lord obscures the future for if he could foresee the events of the next few days his heart would surely fail him. Suddenly, through the walls a loud piercing cry rends the air. He glances, yet again, at the clock, 11.45 a.m.; it has been a long morning. Relief breaks over him in beads of perspiration as, with joy, he learns he is now a father. "Thank you Lord", is all he can say.

On their own at last, father and mother gaze in wonder at the daughter cradled in the mother's arms. Never again will there be just the two of them. There is now a new dimension to their love. The exhausted mother is too excited to sleep as together they revel in the joy that a child has been born, a child much wanted, a child much prayed for, and a child for whom the mother cherishes a promise that she is to rear her for the Lord.

As they gaze in wonder at their child, perfectly formed, and perceive as to family likenesses in her, they remember that for all her apparent innocence, she has been conceived in sin and shapen in iniquity. She needs a Saviour, yes, but knowing the steadfastness of the Lord concerning His promise and believing in His great sovereignty, this thought does not lessen their joy. But what of a name?, this requires little discussion. According to custom the child will be called after her grandmother. An attack of hiccoughs distracts them. There is no one to advise them but inspiration and a little water works wonders and soon the baby is fast asleep.

Two days later the mother is sick, very sick. The doctor has diagnosed puerperal sepsis, or childbed fever as it was better known and the ambulance is on its way. It is a serious disease, from which in

1936, the death rate is very high. Antibiotics are not yet heard of. Transmitted usually by those in attendance at confinement, this communicable and notifiable disease is traced to the midwife. Her previous case had suffered from the same disease, but she did not take her statutory time off.

This information does little to alleviate the anxiety of the over-wrought father, torn as he is by so many conflicting emotions. The mother, while awaiting hospitalisation and between episodes of delirium tries to advise her husband regarding arrangements for the baby. Who will look after the two day old infant? Relatives are many but they are all back home in Lewis. They recount friends likely to assist and eventually agree on one with whom she will be fostered.

Both parents are very upset as their world turns upside down. Early bonding between mother and baby, so necessary to a close relationship will, for the present, be interrupted, but the over-riding concern is for the mother. The father ploughs the depths; he has been told his wife is seriously ill. Will she live? Yet, in their turmoil they believe that this frowning providence is but part of the divinely ordered Plan of the Great Jehovah and they must accept His will. When the parting comes they leave all in the hands of Almighty God.

The husband returns to work. They need the income and it helps to ease the pain and anxiety which constantly fills his life. He visits his daughter, but he feels so helpless as he sees another woman bathe and feed her. Sorrow and concern course through his being as he silently prays to his Lord, almost begging, that the mother's life may be preserved. Worn out he casts himself, his wife and his new born child on the Grace of God and waits .....

The weeks pass ever so slowly and his wife begins to improve. She longs to see her husband, a privilege hitherto denied, and to receive news of her baby. She prays that he may come and as she does the Lord to whom her soul is anchored responds with His Truth. She grasps the promise, believing her request to be granted. He will come and he will be allowed to visit her. She is not disappointed. The preciousness of these moments together are memorable.

Six whole weeks have elapsed since she was first admitted. Now thoughts of home fill her days and she longs to be discharged. Finally, the decision is taken and that day arrives. As she sits by her bedside awaiting the arrival of her husband she reflects on the watchful care of God over His creatures. Their trial has been a sore one but individually they have proved His Eternal love towards them. The wilderness stretches ahead; they know not by what path He will lead them, but they are confident that their God, a sovereign God, will direct and hear them.

The reunion with husband and child can best be described in the words of the Psalmist:

'When Sion's bondage God turn'd back,
As men that dreamed were we
Then filled with laughter was our mouth
Our tongue with melody.'

With the child once more in her arms, the mother's cup of thankfulness overflows. She gazes at the perfection of the tiny fingers clenched tightly in that little hand and thinks "we are fearfully and wonderfully made". Together at family worship that evening they seek to give Him the Glory for His sustaining grace and, committing all to Him, they leave the morrow in His hands.

Unbeknown to them at this time, but not unbeknown to their Lord, is the fact that as a consequence of the infection, their family is complete with their first born. The privilege of bringing another child into the world is no longer theirs. Events are the Lords and the time will come when they will recognise this as His perfect plan for their family. In the meantime they reaffirm their commitment in the words "As for me and my house we will serve the Lord".

chapter three

Childhood Recollections

'Swiftly thus our fleeting days
Bear us down life's rapid stream
Upwards Lord our spirits raise
All below is but a dream.'

Discharging their baptismal vows, the parents seek wisdom to bring up their child in the nurture and admonition of the Lord. This didn't, however, keep the growing child from early manifestations of sinful desires and actions. Indeed correction was often necessary and lessons in obedience hard to learn. As I reflect over this period of my life, much of which is known to me only through others, I can say with St. Augustine, "I acknowledge Thee for the first rudiments of being and my infancy, whereof I remember nothing for Thou hast appointed that man should from others guess much as to himself and believe much on the strength of weak females".

By the time I was two years of age my parents had started to take me regularly to church. I was taught to say my prayers, haltingly at first as I repeated them after my mother. In time the catechism was added to the list of religious learning activities. This I found difficult, for I didn't understand what I was being taught but I believed it because my parents and Sunday School teachers taught it.

We often walked to church in these days and as we did we passed the Salvation Army preaching on the street corner. I would love to have stayed and watched. I was absolutely fascinated by their uniforms, by the large silver instruments of their band on which they boomed out their music and I had often to be dragged away from this simple enjoyment. I was by no means angelic in church and I have often wondered how my parents heard and absorbed the sermon. As I grew older I recall, on coming home from church, being instructed as to the meaning and importance of God's House. I was always told when I was good, I suppose this was meant to encourage me to maintain such behaviour.

Between church services until I was of an age when I could read, I was told Bible stories. These I always enjoyed and I had my favourites. Old testament stories were particularly thrilling. David and Goliath, Daniel in the lion's den, and amazingly, David sparing Saul's life in the cave when he cut off the bottom of Saul's robe. I clearly remember the mental picture I wove around this story and I would ask for it until the time came when I could read it for myself. Sabbath afternoon was always set aside for reading. If either of my parents came across something of special interest they would stop and read the passage aloud to each other. Some of these passages come to mind today, particularly accounts in the 'Men of the Lews' and in the 'Apostle of the North'. These were easier for a child to follow than some passage from a sermon. While my parents read I used to pretend I was a teacher in Sunday School and I would recount the stories I knew. This actually reinforced what I was taught. I cannot recall feeling Sunday long or boring. Keeping the Sabbath day holy was instilled in my mind and to this day I have a peculiar sensitivity towards it. Absolutely nothing unnecessary was undertaken on that day, either by ourselves as a family or by any persons residing in our home. It was the Lord's day and not ours to do with as we pleased. I totally accepted this and the sentiments of the poem which reads:

'A Sabbath well spent brings a week of content
And strength for the toils of the morrow
But a Sabbath profaned what e'er may be gained
Is a certain forerunner of sorrow.'

It is often said that in the homes of the deeply pious, children, through the austerity of the religious aspects of life, often acquire a resentment to spiritual matters. I certainly cannot assent to this. I fully believe that the influence of my God fearing parents and especially my mother with whom I spent most of my time, led me, even at this tender age, to acquire an interest in things spiritual. I can never recollect a time in my life when I didn't want whatever my mother had. I was very aware she was different from the parents of some of the children with whom I mixed at this time, but I never wished her to be anything other than what she was. From childhood through the whole of my life I had a deep respect for her spirituality.

At this time in Glasgow, to eke out the meagre earnings of a shipyard labourer, my mother used to take in lodgers. These were young Island men who came to Glasgow to earn their living. The situation, workwise, in Lewis was very depressed. These men were God fearing and members of the same church. I soon came to love them with childish filial love and they became a big part of the extended family of my life. Their Christian fellowship created a warm aura in our home of which I was to become increasingly aware as I grew older. Without fail, two, sometimes three resided with us. There were two double beds in the bedroom where they slept. My parents slept in the kitchen which had a box-bed fitted into the wall, the curtains of which were drawn together during the day, giving an illusion of a bedless room. Amazingly I cannot recall where I slept and I never thought to ask, but this simple way of living was not lost on me.

These men, together with friends who called, filled my early life with fun and laughter. They played with me, teased me and taught me nursery rhymes, while my mother was kept active preparing meals, laundering the clothes of all these men and darning their socks. 'Yo-yo' and 'Twinkle, Twinkle little star' were great favourites. Reflecting on this time of my life is pleasant. I was a happy, secure child and never complained of boredom or a lack of something to do. When there was no one around I played quite contentedly on my own. Today's children miss out on a stage of their development through the abundance of toys and the constant viewing of television.

At this stage in my development my mother used to recount simple stories from her Island background. These always reflected Christian men and women and were intended to instil a sense of the importance of putting Christ first. Best remembered are two about 'Aonghas-nam-beann' (Angus of the hills) a borderline mentally handicapped man in whom the work of Grace shone so brightly as to be unmistakable. Linking this story to priorities and thankfulness she would recall, 'Angus visited the manse one day and the minister's wife gave him a cup of tea and a slice of bread and jam. To Angus jam was a luxury and he began to cry, "Why are you crying", the minister's wife asked, "do you not like what I have given you?" "Oh!" he sobbed, "I do, but I am afraid I am getting all my good things in this world and I won't get any in the next"'. The other story was about the time he was given some money. As he walked home, he used to say a wee man rose up in his inside and he began to speak to him. "You love the money more than you love Christ, Angus". "I don't" Angus said. "Yes you do, for you keep thinking about it". "Yes, I'm thinking about it" Angus agreed, "but I am thinking about Christ more". "You're making an idol of the money, Angus", the voice went on. "Oh!, bad little man in my inside, be quiet. Look, I will put the money in a hole in the dyke, I can do without it until Monday, but I cannot do without Christ for a single minute". These graphic stories were very impressive and have always remained with me. They have lost nothing in the re-telling.

Gaelic was my only language at this time and yet, it was never a barrier between me and my chum, a boy of my own age who lived in a ground floor flat in the same tenement. We developed our own communication through which we understood our play activities. I never learned more than a word or two of English from him and I am quite certain he never managed even that of Gaelic. For two years we palled around without so much as an argument. Perhaps the Gaelic helped!

The tenement stairs was our favourite location and we were often so absorbed in our make believe games as to be totally unaware of tenants or callers as they tried to pass us. There was one incident when Danny spotted a dead cat in the bin, or midden as we used then to call it, and together we carefully carried it to our wee house on the stair. Our pleasure was short lived for we were observed and marched to our respective homes for a "ticking off" and a wash. That was my first encounter with death and decomposition, but I didn't recognise it. It held no fear, no concern and no awareness, yet I had been taught in a simple way about death and dying, obviously without comprehension for the thought did not establish itself as gloomy. It didn't seem to mean anything. Was I perhaps too young or had it not been adequately explained? I know not. As the natural inclination is away from God and death, I probably shut it out of my thoughts. In the thirties death often claimed young children and my parents would have been failing in their duty had they excluded the subject from their Christian teaching. They certainly stressed the sentiments of a verse I was to read much later in one of my children's books:

'Now that my journey's just begun
My course so little trod
T'were well if ere I further run
My soul were brought to God.'

My happy childhood days were soon to take a serious turn with the outbreak of war. Living next to a fairly large shipyard we were a sitting target for air attack. Although life was about to change dramatically and the atmosphere of the home to become pensive with prayer often ascending, I cannot recall anxiety being in evidence. I developed a healthy respect for the sound of the siren and when it was set off, two short four year old legs hastened up four flights of stairs all eager to announce, "the siren", as if my mother was deaf to the event.

Recollections of being wrapped in a quilt in the middle of the night and carried by my father to the air raid shelter are very clear. Sleepy and disturbed I don't remember crying; I just seemed to accept what was inevitable. One daytime raid is very vivid. My father was at work and my mother took me down to join the other tenants. Some of these women were very afraid and expressed their fear in differing ways. One woman sat with a basin feeling quite nauseous, others sat so quietly they never spoke. Someone suddenly called with much vehemence, "Mrs. Maclean, pray for us". I early learned that it was obvious to them that my mother had a life-line in which they believed in times of crisis as a last resort. Even today I take note of the number of people who in difficulties use the word prayer loosely. How often in newspapers we read of relatives stating "I'm praying she/he will recover", or similar sentiments, when natural disaster strikes. Journalists also refer to prayer from time to time, yet many of these persons do not practice it in their daily lives.

It was a really poignant time, even for a child, when one by one our lodgers were called up for war service. There are things of which I have no recollection, but I heard them often relayed in subsequent years. When the first lodger left for the war, my mother felt very concerned for him in his personal dilemma. She loaned him her favourite book of Spurgeon's sermons assuring him at the same time that he would return safely from the war; but, she added, she couldn't be sure that he would escape injury. He did return, having lost his hand, and my mother was reunited with Spurgeon's sermons. An exceedingly precious book to her, she always read it and I recall her saying in later life that she never opened its pages without receiving a blessing for her soul. I now have this book, duly inscribed with the lodger's name and home address, which was his way of ensuring it wouldn't get lost during war travel. Both he and my mother are now within the Celestial City and that book is as precious to me as it once was to them.

Rigid regulations were imposed by the Government of the day regarding gas masks and the 'black-out'. The purpose for which these were designed was not understood by me, but while the reality of the black-out did not affect me, the gas mask filled me with rigid fear. I will never forget the day my mother took me by tram car to the Govan school to be kitted out with my gas mask. Even as I write I can see all these different sizes of fearful looking apparitions. Someone came up with one for me to try on. That did it. No way would I go near it. Absolutely terrified I didn't just cry, I became quite hysterical. The mission was not a success, but my mother did leave with the boxed product. Whoever said that 'the element of human happiness is very slender, the small things often perturbing our happiness more than the near calamities', spoke well. I was more afraid of that small gas mask than of all the enemy aircraft which filled our skies.

Our home was certainly a guarded house the night a nearby shipyard was targetted and bombing was heavy. All the tenement windows suffered damage or were cracked except those of our flat. God's protection was in evidence the next morning...

'... and from her lips to Heaven above
A fervent prayer arose
That God would raise a wall around
And save them from their foes ...
... I prayed for God's preserving care
But recollect, my son
Nought is impossible with Him
He speaks and it is done.'

With these events life in Glasgow was about to end. Children were now being evacuated to the country, but for us the decision was taken to return to Lewis to my maternal grandmother's home, my father remaining in Glasgow to earn our living. Truly life was in turmoil. It is said that the dark seasons afford the sweetest and strongest manifestations of the power of faith. My parents, once more, could but hold fast the word of promise. That God reigned was their abiding comfort. None-the-less, for my father there must have ensued a period of incredible loneliness. Letter mail was erratic owing to the vagaries of war and the telephone was a rare commodity. Compelled to leave her husband in war torn Glasgow with its grim history of destruction, my mother's heart must have been filled with sorrow. But their experience was not an isolated one; thousands throughout the country were facing the same reality, some in hope, some in despondency. As for me, a child in the centre of all these uncertainties, I remained undisturbed. Going to Lewis was an exciting prospect.

The move to the Island was expected to be a temporary one. My mother and I would return to Glasgow when the war was over. Our thoughts are not His thoughts. We never did. I was to be a teenager before we were a family unit again. 'He doeth according to His Will in the Army of Heaven, and among the inhabitants of the earth: none can stay His hand or say unto Him, What doest Thou?'

chapter four

Growing Pains

'Moments swiftly fly away
Nothing can compel their stay'.

In the early forties the journey to Lewis was not one to be enjoyed but rather one to be endured. Crossing over from Mallaig via Kyle meant some seven hours at sea. The Minch, notorious for its squally conditions when the wind blew fresh, was at best uncomfortable. Plying its waters was the Loch Ness. Built for practicality rather than ease, berths were few and outwith the means of many of her passengers. Second best were the narrow mattress-like berths. These were loaned cheaply and carried on to the deck where they were laid side by side, giving the impression that travellers were packed like sardines. Warm clothing and travelling rugs together with flasks of tea and sandwiches are my early recollections of travel necessities.

Transporting passengers from Glasgow to Mallaig was a coal driven train. It chug-chugged out of Queen Street station, hooter blaring loudly, with columns of black smoke arising from the furnace funnel to blow across the carriage windows as a white cloud blotting out the scene. The City rolled behind; at last we were on our way.

This part of the journey was for me the least desirable. Long and tedious, it added another seven hours to our travel and while I remember little of sea crossings in these tender years, I do remember the train. The unpleasant smell of coal fumes circulating the corridor and carriages is still vivid in my memory. Yet, despite stops at the many stations en route, as with all else in life, pleasant or unpleasant, it eventually passed. Destination was finally a reality.

Of Mallaig I remember little except the fishy smell of boats tied up in the harbour, fish boxes and barrels and what seemed like hundreds of squawking seagulls. I never saw so many in my life. As we walked from the train to the mail-boat, laden as we were with suitcases and parcels it was hoped that the airborne missiles descending around us, with no respect for person or possession, could be avoided. Almost as offensive as gas warfare, I cannot recall either myself or my mother ever being targetted. A truly remarkable feat!

Always welcome, as we returned our plinths to the purser, were the distant lights of Stornoway. Dim by comparison with what is known to us today, they none-the-less beamed out to sea. At first no more than the twinkle of stars, but they beckoned us to our homeland. Interestingly though our residence was in Glasgow, in common with many Lewis exiles, the Island was always home.

A quick tidy up and we join the long queue of passengers, many leaning over the side of the ship from quarter-deck to forecastle, craning in an effort to see loved ones. The ship docks, the wooden gangway is hauled into position and tied securely, and we passengers disembark. My mother glances around, encourages her restless daughter to stay close and begins walking towards the 'boat's bus', so called by direct translation from the Gaelic. We pass MacBrayne's office and the fish mart; my mother stops to adjust her heavy load and gives a word of encouragement to her flagging five year old, by now finding everything a bit strange and so at last, with luggage on board, we take our seats on the bus. There are the inevitable delays while we await passengers who have nipped into the nearby hotel but we finally get under way. Another thirty minutes and we are home.

Life in Lewis, novel to begin with, was soon replaced by feelings of homesickness for the father left behind in Glasgow. In common with most girls, this little girl had been a real daddy's pet and she did not yet possess the powers of intellect to grasp the disturbances war had occasioned within the family unit. Hitler meant nothing to her, while the household talk of the fighting forces defending the country washed over her. But ration books, clothing coupons and the black-out were, even to a child, tangible realities of the times. Rationing was an interesting system; essential provisions were available but luxuries, even if affordable, were in short supply.

During the communion time my grandmother's house used to be full of visitors from surrounding congregations. Rationing then proved a testing time for the family. But God never let his children down and as in the case of the widow of Zarephath the barrel of meal did not waste nor the cruise of oil fail. There was always adequate provision even if tea and sugar required careful distribution to make them last. I remember a children's book which was being read to me at this time, referring to the Bible as the Christian's ration book, the safekeeping of it was in the heart, the coupons were short prayers from the Bible such as, "Give us this day our daily bread" or "God be merciful to me a sinner". Yes, the war taught - even a child.

Home was now shared with my grandmother and two unmarried aunts. My mother and I were allocated the end room in the house. This was turned into a bedsit and had the advantage of having a porch with an external door opening off it. This porch acted as kitchen and so we could enjoy in a measure our own privacy. How I missed the fun of standing on a stool in my hand-knitted skirt and jumper, sleeves rolled up, by my way of it, helping my mother with the washing up. More likely keeping her back! I loved the sink and the running water but this commodity was no longer available. I had to learn to ration water, drawn as it was in buckets from the well. This was especially so on Sunday for on the Lord's Day water was never drawn. Another privilege denied was the light at the end of a switch. This was not quite such a hardship, for the oil lamps, wicks regularly trimmed, gave off a soft glow and a not unpleasant odour of paraffin. The tilly lamp, on the other hand, was a great improvement lightwise and one soon became accustomed to its steady hum. Life was certainly different but a child quickly adapts and quickly accepts situations which cannot be changed and in any case there were many compensatory factors.

School was another experience. Never will I forget that memorable first day when my mother, on taking me to school, left me at the mercy of the infant teacher. With lower lip trembling I longed to run after her, but pride gritted my teeth and instead I turned to survey the motley crowd around me. There were big ones, wee ones, fat ones, thin ones, some in pigtails, some with ringlets or short hair, some curly, some straight, boys with short trousers and tweed wool knee socks and jumpers and strong ankle boots; girls in tweed skirts or pinafores with blouses and jumpers. As I surveyed them, they looked me up and down wondering who the stranger in the camp may be. They were known to each other, but I hadn't been long enough in the Island to have become acquainted with them. I felt isolated and lonely. But how did my mother feel as she walked the mile back home with no child by her side? The quietness which met her as she entered the room we knew as home must have given rise to much reflective thought. My teacher had been her teacher - she could well recall the unyielding firmness - but at least I didn't have to carry a peat to school every day to keep the fire burning as was the case with the children of her day, and I had shoes on my feet, a luxury which many could not afford then. I must count my blessings.

School life had now indeed begun but I cannot look back with any great affection on this period. Firstly, I had to build up relationships with other children. My pre-school experiences had been so different from theirs and in this there were great knowledge gaps between us. In the thirties and forties few children left these Island shores until they were required to do so in order to earn their living. During day hours I recognised a bus as a bus but after nightfall when buses travelled with lights on I referred to them as trains or trams. I was never allowed to forget an occasion when my granny was in Stornoway for the day, a big event in these times. She had promised to buy me a pair of shoes and I stood by the window looking out into the dark winter's night impatiently waiting for her return. At last the bus stopped at the gate and I excitedly jumped up and down shouting, "the train has stopped". But there were far more fundamental differences and these were not outgrown as other childish ones were. In fact they became more firmly entrenched in my thoughts and life and were obvious to my school mates. For example, when we fell into argument, or squabbled or, yes, even fought, as children do, a more humiliating nickname than 'Holy' could not be found for me. Had they but realised how far off the mark they really were! But it did speak volumes for the home influence and my own early inclinations.

Conscious of the fact that the teacher had favourites and that I was not numbered among them added to the stress of these early experiences. I was not a lover of gymnastics, but I did enjoy playground games and the childish races of the annual sports day. When this, however, was taken into account with my classroom performance, it showed that I never seemed to excel at anything. Average, I was labelled. I greatly missed the home influence and longed for the day when I was old enough to leave school. I carried this attitude into secondary school, though I much preferred it to primary. At least here I was good at something, for I always got the 'star' in domestic science and my bent was, therefore, towards an occupation in which I could use these skills. I classify myself as a poor scholar and emphasise this in order that the Lord may be given all the credit for later achievements. Without Him I could do nothing.

While I was at primary school, the walk home was deemed too far at lunch-break and so arrangements were made for me to lunch nearby with family friends. On one occasion when asked what I had had for lunch my response was short, "bull", I said. Mystified, my mother went on to question me further about this delicacy, but my replies left her none the wiser. Eventually it became known that what I had eaten was salt salmon, salt being the only means of preserving food as electricity was still unknown in the villages. Of course a child could not be entrusted with such a profound secret as to how households procured salmon! It had to be disguised in case I might disclose it to my school friends.

As I grew older I was required to assist with chores suited to my years. At first there were the simple tasks such as dusting and polishing. I had a passion for dolls and playing 'little houses' with my chum and so these tasks, which had to take priority, seemed as drudgery. Later I had to help with the harvesting and peat cutting activities. This was great fun to begin with, but when these became a responsibility the fun element soon evaporated.

A large hill divided our croft in two. A narrow path hewn in the rock by my grandfather permitted walking access for his family, but it was quite impossible to drive a horse and cart and the cattle up and over this route. The land-court therefore sanctioned access on the adjoining croft. Tractor power was not yet a reality and the horse and cart had long since been parted with. My grandfather had died many years before this, and so there were no male members to manage the croft or lead the horse with cart or plough. Nonetheless, the necessities of living, in these hard and depressed times, required the continuance of crofting activities. Cattle, sheep and hens were part of the family economy and so the land must be tilled and the harvest gathered.

Most of the arable land lay beyond this hill and so two aunts, my mother and I walked to and fro to the shore - an inlet of the sea bordered the end of the croft - to tend potatoes and engage in hay-making. In due time these commodities were transported on our backs to the homestead, along the access referred to. This was a tedious performance. The loads of hay were secured in a special way so that they would not fall apart as we journeyed, but there was no way of preventing the rope from digging into the biceps.

Unless it is an illusion, the weather appeared to be kinder in these days. Even the little midge made her debut later. Peat carting time and late harvest are my recollections of the little rascals. Perhaps the drier summer climate kept them at bay. Our people depended much on good weather. Prayer was often wont to be made and the promise, 'while the earth remaineth, seedtime and harvest, and cold and heat, and summer and winter and day and night shall not cease', was claimed. The Lord was faithful to His promise.

Another not to be forgotten activity was peat cutting and drying. Still a major form of fuel, much of the hard work has been removed with the advent of tractors which, in many instances, take the dried peat straight from the peat bank. This fuel, supplemented as it now is with electricity and gas, is used for cooking and heating. As it burns it gives off a distinctive reek often remarked upon by tourists.

Peat-cutting is an activity not easily undertaken by one person. Neighbours, therefore, assisted one another, but in those days of few vehicles, all the edibles had to be conveyed to the moor. Prepared in advance, the three course lunch, afternoon tea and evening meal were carefully packed into a creel which the woman of the house carried on her back. Water for tea, pans, utensils and dishes were all transported. A fire was lit to heat the food and water. When it is considered that women had often to walk great distances into the moor with these commodities and also share in the cutting and throwing of the wet turf, it will be realised that their work was indeed exhaustive. To us children it was great fun. I loved the wide open moors and there were other families with children engaged upon the same activities.

My father's leave was taken up with carting the peats home. Back and fore he walked with a hired horse and cart, from early morning till late evening, for many days, until the peats were all brought home. In the meantime, my mother and I remained on the moor to assist with loading the cart. This mode of transport had enormous limitations. The cart carried such a small quantity of peat and the horse had to be led and never taken off the main rough peat road for fear that the cart might sink in the soft earth. The peats were therefore taken in sacks from the peat bank, again on our backs, to the roadside. This could take as long as a week. Once home they were then skilfully stacked to prevent water seepage during the winter. One can imagine how truly this generation entered into the spirit of Thanksgiving Thursday as they lifted up their hearts in gratitude to God for His care over the harvest and other seasonal work.

The hard labour paid off, for the basic necessities of this simple life were now assured for another year. Milk, cream, butter, crowdie, eggs and meat were all home produce, a well balanced and healthy diet. I can readily recall, after milking time, white enamel basins being filled with milk and set aside in a special cupboard awaiting the separation of the cream. It was then lifted off with a cleansed scallop shell and set aside for butter making. Sometimes the temptation to taste the cream was too great and the evidence of my yielding to the temptation could not be hid. The scolding for sticking a finger in the basin seemed worth it at the time. I hadn't then learned the text, 'Thou God seest me'. But we had our yogurts, thick milk after the cream was removed, and our milk shakes, oatmeal, cream and thick milk mixed together. Though not of course then known by these names, they were delicacies in their own right.

A day came when I graduated to filling bobbins. One aunt earned her living by weaving Harris Tweed. A home industry, the production of this fabric was then at its zenith and the cloth was in great demand. The Orb stamp proved the authenticity of its handwoven quality. Both loom and bobbin machine were foot operated, but pedalling too fast was unproductive as the soft yarn broke very easily. For my share in this work I earned the princely sum of ten shillings per tweed. I thought it was a fortune when I received it, but Oh! it took such a long time to earn. Watching the shuttles of the loom as they shot the threads of the weft between the thread of the warp was at first interesting, but it soon became boring through familiarity and I used to think, "I never want to be a weaver".

When I was ten years old my grandmother died. This is my first recollection of a family bereavement and the days leading up to the funeral rest vividly in my memory. Grannie seemed such an old person, but then grannies did in those days. Her face, puckered by age and worn by hard work, and her long black clothes did nothing to enhance her appearance, particularly in the eyes of a child. Yet, I had a great affection for her as she sat at her spinning wheel, twisting yarn from which she made socks and other knitwear for selling. Her providence had been hard. She lost her mother when she was eight years of age and had to help care for her brothers and sister until her father remarried. Her husband was invalided for many years and died young and her four sons left to seek employment on the other side of the world. Two of them were subsequently lost in a canoeing accident in Mexico before I was born.

By the age of twenty-one my grandmother had met and married my grandfather. It wasn't easy in these days for someone from the south east of the Island to meet someone from the south west but God finds His own way to bring His providence to fruition. My grandfather at this time was a policeman based in the south-east of the Island and my grandmother, according to the custom and necessity of the times, used to walk the distance between her home and this locality to gather lichen off the rocks. From this substance a home dye was produced with which the fleeces of wool were dyed and then spread on the fences to dry in readiness for carding. She was later to find employment in Stornoway as a domestic servant which is where she was at the time of her marriage.

In due course my grandparents returned to my grandfather's native village and the family croft. Their circumstances appear to have been better than many of their contemporaries, as the ruins of their home and barn confirm. There were two separate dwellings facing each other about twenty feet apart. These dwellings were each of two rooms. The barn housed the cattle in one end, the dividing partition separating them from the hay, corn and feeding stuffs. The family home consisted of a kitchen/living area and a bedroom and here eight healthy children were reared. A spring well, sunk nearby, from which the household and the cattle had their water supply, was covered to prevent access to the animals. This well was still functional in my early years and water was drawn from it to fill the sheep dipping tank.

In the late nineteenth and early twentieth centuries, many homes in the townships of those and other islands permitted cattle-housing. This meant that the dwelling housed cattle in one end and the family in the other. There was a common entrance. This mode of dwelling held a very high public health risk and it is quite amazing that the neo-natal mortality rates were not higher. Certainly deaths were frequent with infants dying from, 'galar na coig oidhche' (the disease of the five nights). The principal cause, not then understood, was undoubtedly neo-natal tetanus. Spores gained entry in all probability through the umbilical cord.

I remember visiting these communal dwellings in my younger days. Much improved of course, there were still a few occupied in the forties. For all their insanitary living conditions, these stone and lime houses were amazingly cosy within. The living room was about twelve feet square and contained a few chairs, a wooden bench, a dresser for the dishes and a table. Occasionally it also housed a bed. A small iron stove replaced the open fire, but as the fuel door often remained open for added warmth and cheer, smoke frequently curled into the room.

An upward glance would reveal what looked like icicles of soot hanging from the roof beams. Two small windows in the thatch roofing permitted daylight. The walls were plastered with clay and whitewashed, or in some instances papered, while the floor was swept bare or covered with linoleum. The bedroom opened off the living room and contained two, sometimes, three box beds, arranged alongside the room. Wooden roofing sloped gently towards the wall to prevent rain seepage through the thatch finding its way on to the bed. A cured deerskin graced the floor. It was primitive in the extreme, yet, warm neighbourliness, goodwill towards each other and adherence towards Christian principles and godliness, marked the inhabitants. Here parents taught their children the rudiments of Christianity while their example, in such deprivation, declared to them the sovereign God who was central in their lives. They were undoubtedly poor in material things, but in their simple living there was togetherness and a richness in the things of God.

Reference has already been made to the fact that my grandmother came from a different part of the Island. This meant that at communion time the home was a hive of activity as visitors from her native part resided with her for the weekend. It was the custom and still is, for Christians from adjoining congregations to attend communion wherever it is held. Distance and lack of transport was no barrier, but it meant that visitors required to stay for the duration of the services. These services extended from Thursday through to Monday. Thursday, known as Fast Day, is a day of humiliation and prayer. In the era considered it was treated almost like the Lord's Day. No unnecessary work was undertaken. Even today many shops, banks, offices and schools remain closed. Friday is known as Question Day. Male communicant members from different congregations are invited to address the question - a verse of scripture given out by an office bearer or male member from the congregation in which the communion is held. Marks or tokens of the true believer are sought. These men frequently make reference to their testimony and their subsequent experiences in the life of grace. It is intended to be a means of encouragement for young believers who have not yet made public profession of their faith. Saturday's services are preparatory while on the Lord's Day morning, the Lord's supper is dispensed. The evening service is evangelical and many unconverted, young and not so young, attend. Monday is thanksgiving and the close of the feast.

Up and over the rocky hill at the back of the old house these godly men and women could be seen twice every day as they journeyed to and from church. At that time church was some distance from the houses and often they arrived with wet clothes, a fact to which they seemed oblivious in their conversation of matters spiritual. But wet clothes must be dried in readiness for the next service and this could only be done by the fireside. The prepared meal was then set before the guests, enhanced by a grace which flowed from deep thankfulness. Midnight often found these lovely Christians pouring out their hearts in rich spiritual experience. So united in communion were they with their Lord, so instructed in doctrine, so ardent in love that they made a deep impression on the growing children. Each morning and evening their devotions at family worship could be heard. The rich melodious singing of the psalms in Gaelic echoed in the hills around the home. These were wonderful occasions and the girls in particular were eager to help with the advance preparations, white washing, wallpapering, extra cleaning and cooking. Great excitement attended these events. I have often wondered where they all slept, but they did. Poor they may have been in the rewards of the world, but they were richly endowed in the treasures of Redemption.

I used to hear my mother in later life recount these memories of her childhood, while I sat enthralled listening and picturing the scene. I was left with the distinct impression that these devout men and women had an extraordinary relationship with their Lord. In fellowship and communion with Him, they knew the joy of their salvation. Their earthly priorities were in the correct order and they were not uptaken with secular activities as our generation is, much to our spiritual disadvantage.

I was never part of the home setting to which reference has just been made. When we returned from Glasgow my grandmother had long since moved into the home in which we were offered refuge. One of the uncles, who in the nineteen twenties went to South America in search of a living, arranged the construction of the house which was to be the family home for the next fifty years. It was built nearer the main road, on the opposite side of the hill which dominated the croft, making for easier access except during harvesting. If death deprived my grandmother of her mother at a tender age, it was soon to remove three of her four sons who went to South America, one from tuberculosis and two to whom reference has already been made. 'The Lord gave and the Lord taketh away'. While the family could say this, their human hearts bled. My mother seldom spoke of her brothers. Even before their deaths, the departure, on the brink of manhood, to a country so far removed was an unforgettable wrench. They did return to the Island home on one or two occasions, but the journey was by sea and very long and conditions were difficult. Married life was to separate them still further as they settled down in a foreign land.

I recall hearing of an amusing occurrence during a visit to the homestead by the one surviving son. Accompanied by his wife and two daughters, none of whom could speak English, he was overheard to say to his Spanish/Argentinian wife one Sunday morning that he had forgotten to shave on Saturday night. Shaving was not considered among the works of necessity and therefore not undertaken on the Lord's Day. The elder daughter, however, decided she would resolve the problem and unbeknown to the household she went out of doors and allowed the hens to escape. It was the corn planting season when it was customary to secure the hens in the hen house to prevent the destruction of the newly sown seed. Excitedly she returned indoors and by gestures and unknown language tried to explain to her grandmother that the hens were in the fields. It was something the children had been warned against doing. I'm sure it was as well she never understood the ticking off directed at her by her grandmother. In the confusion which ensued, while aunts and grandmother rounded up the hens, a dish of hot water from the kettle on the stove was taken to her father's bedroom and the daily shaving routine performed. I was reminded of this story on a recent visit to Brazil. At the time I was only one year old and we were of course staying in Glasgow. At least one uncle never shared the sentiments of his forefathers in relation to the sanctity of the Lord's Day.

After my grandmother's death, my aunt handed me ten pounds, being a sum of money my grannie had left me. Never having handled so much money before, I jumped up and down excitedly shouting, "I'm rich, I'm rich". How times have changed! I think I must have blocked out my grannie's death for I cannot recall my reaction nor the days beyond her funeral. I do remember attending one of the wakes and sitting with a neighbour totally mesmerised by all the people gathered. This neighbour took me to the room and asked me to place my hand on the coffin, telling me not to be frightened. I was then taken by her to her home until after the funeral and there rests my memory.

About this time my father took a break from his work. Up until now we only saw him for two weeks each year during the Glasgow fair fortnight. Oh! the thrill when he came home. This is when I felt my first childish pangs of jealousy as I saw him kissing my mother before myself. I never could understand that his relationship with my mother was closer than with myself. The presents were wonderful, making all the absences temporarily worthwhile. Part of the fun, of course, was showing them off to my chums. They couldn't understand an absent father nor the wonderful joy of seeing him again and having him home. This time, however, was different, his extended leave was in order to build us a home of our own.

What anticipation was ours when the house was finally completed and ready for us to move in. All the furniture which had been part of early childhood and held in store was now unpacked and graced our still humble dwelling, only two rooms and a kitchen. We still had no electricity or running water, but we did have a sink. What bliss! No longer did we require to go outside to dispose of waste water products. That in itself was a bonus and greatly appreciated. How much we now take for granted! The small things of life are no longer great.

This house holds many memories. Here in the privacy of her own home I would find my mother on her knees in the bedroom pouring out her heart in language heard and understood in heaven. I would come home from school to find her there and I would just quietly close the door and come away. I never resented it, it was so very natural. I was aware that she was wrestling in audience with her Lord. She had a deep sense of devotion to the things of God and I had nothing but respect for her. If I slipped out before morning worship to meet up with my friend, we would both be beckoned indoors while she read and prayed and called on us both to say the Lord's prayer. Her desire to ground me well in the things of God met with response, for it never did provoke rebellion, but rather created within me a renewed desire to obtain whatever she had, for it seemed so right to me. Throughout my childhood and teens I observed how her face glowed with sheer pleasure when the Lord's people gathered in our home. I was also aware of the fact that she and they laughed with an almost holy laughter during their time together. Job speaks of God filling the mouth with laughter and the lips with rejoicing, but at the time I knew this not. The scene filled me many times with a longing to know the God of their salvation, for knowing Him made them so obviously happy. I have to say though, that there were times when I took advantage of the fellowship in our home. I was very interested in reading and I often buried myself in my books so that I did not always hear my mother call on me to make the tea.

The year I left school both my parents were unwell and I was required to remain at home for the first week after the school break. We had a cow and by this time I was milking and feeding her. I had been anxious to perform this task which fascinated me and as our snow white cow was so docile it was agreed. She had no tickle in her udder, therefore, it was not necessary to tie her hind legs to prevent her from spilling the milk, if she became restless. A zinc pail containing her bran feed was placed before her and while she ate and later licked the pail, I would proceed to milk, first with a tin jug milking one teat with one hand and then, as I became more proficient, using both hands to milk two teats straight into an enamel bucket. This halving of milking time was a boon because, as with all routine tasks, monotony soon set in. When the week was up I decided not to return to school. This information was communicated to the Rector.

At the time I was but fifteen years of age, yet, I felt mature and on the brink of adulthood. I had no ambition, no knowledge as to how I was to earn my living nor even any thought of it and I had no desire to leave home. There were no career officers to guide us. Being an only child, I loved children and hoped one day that I might mother several.

Beyond this I had no vision. I sought no worldly pleasures and had no interest whatsoever in social activities. I couldn't even imagine these exciting any pleasure. I never went to the pictures, as we called the cinema, to dances or to parties, excepting Hallowe'en when I was a child. The significance of Hallowe'en was not then understood. It was just a party for the children held in different homes each year. I did go to a few house weddings, as was the custom of these times. The whole village would be invited to the wedding and the days prior to the event were full of activity as the women prepared and cooked large quantities of chicken and lamb. There was always a three course meal after which we were given a portion of bride's cake. This, we youngsters were asked to place under our pillow, to help us to dream. Of what? I am unsure. But for us the most exciting part was the reading of the telegrams and the delivery of speeches. As we listened we all gazed longingly at the beautiful dresses and hoped that one day we too might wear a similar dress. Beyond the wedding I never once paused to think what marriage meant. There was absolute naivety.

After one such wedding I went with a friend to the village hall to attend the wedding dance. The Scottish dance music could be heard at some distance, while, as we approached, the patter of feet resounded on the wooden floor. I felt a reluctance to enter. Once in I took one look at the activites around me and said to my friend "I cannot stay here for I feel that Satan himself is present". It was a very interesting reaction for I had never considered where I stood spiritually. I merely knew I wanted, as I always did, to cast in my lot with the Lord's people. I was aware that my desires and interests were at variance with my friends. I knew I was different, but if this difference was more than the influence of my upbringing, I knew not. Whether a believer or not I couldn't stay in that dance hall that night. It was as impossible as the thought that man would one day walk on the moon. My friend tried to dissuade me by suggesting, "You cannot possibly walk home alone past the cemetery". I knew I could. The cemetery held no fear, the dance hall did. That girl forsook her own pleasure and accompanied me the two miles home. As far as I am aware she is still not a Christian.

My father had by now returned to Lewis permanently. His folks came from the extreme north of the Island and occasionally we would visit them, usually remaining two or three nights. Few owned cars, but public transport existed and it was not too difficult to travel. However; by virtue of infrequent contact, for telecommunication was rare, I was never to establish very close ties with my paternal relatives. By the time I was born both grandparents had died and this further affected the loosening of the ties. With the exception of my father, his family were never to influence the experiences of my life. I came to know them best through the many stories my father would relate during the long winter evenings. I loved my father dearly and through him his family.

One evening in early autumn as the sun set behind the hills and the swans rested on the loch beside our home, I considered the chain of events which moulded my life, without giving much thought to the fact that it was all part of God's plan for my life. School days had ended and the relief was enormous. I didn't have a care in the world. I felt content to spend the rest of my life cooking, sewing, reading and of course, sharing in all the other chores of rural life. I never as much as thought whether devotion to practicality would last. If someone had suggested what the future held I would have been perplexed to the point of disbelief. A reserved, unlettered girl rising to leadership? Impossible. But what is impossible to man is possible to God. I must await the unfolding of events. In the meantime, I could not foresee that my life would radically change and my pleasure day by day, drawn, as it was, from the simple life that I led with my parents, satisfied.

chapter five

Fashioning The Clay

'How are they esteemed as earthern pitchers, the work of the hands of the potter!'

'**I**n the beginning God'. I was early to learn this, though I remained mystified as to the infinitude of God. A God without beginning was difficult to comprehend, yet, interestingly, I did believe it. Not because I could reason it out, I couldn't, but because the Bible said it and my parents and Sunday School teachers taught it. A God without end I had less difficulty with because, again, I had been taught that, on death, His children would be forever with Him in an endless eternity. Did not the Shorter Catechism teach that, 'The souls of believers are at their death made perfect in holiness and do immediately pass into Glory, and their bodies, being still united to Christ, do rest in their graves until the resurrection'. The body, resting in the grave and returning to dust was perplexing, yet, I believed that God had created me from the dust of the earth and I believed He had created all mankind and the beasts of the field by the same process. How? I never even thought to reason, I simply believed it. Did God not say? 'Let the earth bring forth the living creature after his kind', and then, 'the Lord God formed man of the dust of the earth'.

Reflecting on the process of spiritual knowledge during this period of my life, I can but say that its growth seemed commensurate with the differing stages of my normal development from childhood through teenage years and into adulthood. Learning is an active principle which continues throughout our lifetime, but I'm sure this dawning comprehension is the experience of many. It stands to reason that as we grow older so too must our capacity for knowledge increase.

During this challenging period, quite inadvertently, my thoughts were confused by my mother. I had a particular dislike for maggots - I still do - and confrontation with them made me cringe and quickly move away. My mother had no such inhibitions. In her working life as cook to the aristocracy of her day, game and particularly venison, was required to hang until the maggots dropped off. This culinary delight was then considered ready for cooking. Observing my reaction she would quietly remind me that the day would come when I would call the maggot and the earth worm 'my sister'. This set me thinking again on the relationship between my body and the earth and yet I never once thought of a process of decay which made this both possible and feasible and no one explained it to me until a number of years later when I had entered the nursing profession. Sometimes I think, that when we talk with youngsters we take their knowledge base for granted and expect them to understand without explanation.

This thought about the creatures of the earth obviously remained with me, for when later I took up rock and trout fishing I used to dig the garden for bait. The common round worm was my quest and when I picked up this wriggly creature I never failed to remember my mother's words. Allowing the earth to trickle through my fingers I thought, this is what I am made of, this, in the process of time is that to which I will return and, yes, the worm will inhabit the same space, the same earth. I never knew then that Job had said, 'though after my skin worms destroy this body, yet in my flesh shall I see God'. Were these thoughts morbid? No. I never reflected on them to this end and neither did I permit my thoughts to dwell upon the subject of the grave for too long. Why? With hindsight I know it was because I doubted my eternal salvation. I had no sense of assurance. I was in bondage. I had had no conversion experience. No 'before or after' and I couldn't believe I was a Christian saved by grace. Thus I grew up, the word of God permeating my thoughts and my life's experiences, even if in an infantile and preliminary way.

Though unaware of it I was now about to enter the working phase of my life. I had often heard the words, 'In the sweat of thy brow thou shalt eat bread', a consequence of the fall, it was a command and a promise. How was this to be fulfilled in my life? I was still carefree, still content to work at home helping my parents, still without direction for my life, still only a young teenager. All this was soon to change. God's providence is meticulous, His timing perfect and as potter He must needs fashion His clay.

"Mrs. MacKay called today", my mother said as I entered the back door, "she wants you to work for her during the season". The response was expected to be in the affirmative, if at all. Work was work and there was no consideration as to suitability. My mother helped out from time to time in this household and so I was not entirely unfamiliar with the terrain or the woman I was to serve, yet I arrived there in trepidation. Another maid, some years my senior, worked with me while a Land Army woman was engaged on farming duties. We were all very busy, yet it was a happy time and we enjoyed some congenial fellowship together. Home was little over a mile away and I used to walk there whenever I had a few hours off. This was as much off duty as we expected, other than a Sunday evening to attend church. Work always came first. The wage for such employment was low, but in our small family it was helpful and for me it was useful grounding. So began my first job, which in this particular field was to be my last. Not because I wished it to be so. I had no incentives otherwise and leisure was comparative. 'Man proposes, God disposes'. The season over I was back home.

At this time I used to help out in the manse during the communion season. This was always a thrilling experience. I loved being among the Lord's people and counted it a great privilege to be associated with them. Two particular visiting ministers come before my mind, even as I write. I felt such warmth towards them, an attachment I could not understand. I was still only sixteen or seventeen years of age and these saintly ministers seemed so old; indeed, one was very elderly, probably in his seventies at the time. They never fussed over me or conversed much with me, yet, their godly demeanour spoke volumes and when on the Monday evening they left the Island shores for their congregations on the Scottish mainland, I felt quite homesick after them. What drew me? With hindsight I believe it was the agape love by which we are to recognise that we have passed from death unto life. 'We know that we have passed from death unto life because we love the brethren'.

On one particular evening prior to the service, my own minister spoke with me of the need to see myself as the chief of sinners. I believed I did and so I argued back, possibly giving myself away. I was not unfamiliar with the term 'the chief of sinners'. Years before I had seen these words, 'This is a faithful saying and worthy of all acceptation that Jesus Christ came into the world to save sinners, of whom I am chief', emblazoned across the page of a children's story book and they made an indelible impression. My minister seemed convinced in his opinion of me and I went to church deeply troubled and very confused. I heard little of the service that evening as in tears I tried to pray and establish my salvation. I had no spiritual enlightenment, nothing which would clarify for me the path upon which I was travelling. This caused me great anguish, especially when I heard the brethren on Question Day relate their experiences. This wonderful peace which invaded their souls when they passed from death unto life was something I longed after and its absence made me question whether I was really a believer. I could only testify to a yearning after things spiritual which had commenced as far back in childhood as memory would go. This led to periods of doubt when I seemed only to proceed from one spiritual confusion to another and was to result in my reaction the night I was told I had cancer.

Returning to the period when I helped in the manse, a visitor once addressed me and enquired as to what career I intended pursuing. Before I could reply, the minister, who was within earshot, responded, "Oh! Chrissie is going to be a philosopher", and he laughed in his inimitable way. The lady proceeded no further. I never forgot the incident and not knowing at that time what a philosopher did or was I consulted the pocket dictionary when I returned home. Amused, my mother and I read, 'A wise man'. Well, that I couldn't accomplish. A larger dictionary left us none the wiser. 'One who studies phenomena ... with practical wisdom and calmness of temper'. I knew neither.

Actually, I never did understand the sentiments behind this statement and the prophesy remains unfulfilled! Yes, these were wonderful times on which I look back with fond memories, but they were also enlightening.

One evening at home as I lay on the sofa reading a missionary book I was suddenly consumed with a desire to become a missionary and serve in Africa. I did not consider this a call to Christian service nor was I filled with a passion for souls. I don't know how well I understood either. I simply knew of a deep longing to help in that country. What could I do? My thoughts were by now settled on a course in domestic science and my expectation was, in the fullness of time, to attend such a course in Aberdeen. My parents were reluctant to see me go though they understood the necessity for me to leave home. I too was having my own difficulties and I kept putting the decision off. Now I had a further complication. Only this time the desire was so strong that my parents temporarily ceased to figure in my thoughts. What could I do in Africa with a domestic science qualification? Nothing, I thought, so what could I do? I read that nurses were called for. Could I be a nurse? I never even paused to debate the question. I had no idea what nursing entailed. I never considered whether I had the physique, I had never stepped inside a hospital, I had no relatives who were nurses, but I determined that this is what I must do. The more I thought of it the more I was convinced of my decision until ultimately I told my parents. I never mentioned Africa but merely that I was going to embark on a nurse training programme. The reaction was not what I expected. Instead of being encouraged I was positively discouraged. I could never be a nurse, I was told. I didn't have the required education etcetera. This made me all the more determined to achieve my objective. I made application, I was interviewed and I was accepted. Still, there was resistance at home, but on the 17th of May 1954, two and a half months short of my eighteenth birthday, I commenced training in what was to be my life's work. It was the first step in the fulfilment of God's plan for my future.

The then General Nursing Council had agreed on affiliation between the Island hospital and Glasgow Royal Infirmary. This entailed a four year training programme, yet, many Island girls took advantage of this package to remain in close proximity with their home for as long as possible. I was among these.

After four months revelling in the title nurse I was transferred to another ward. Here I had the privilege of assisting in the nursing care of one of our Island ministers, a giant in the faith. I remained in awe of his presence whenever I approached his bedside. Silly really, for a gentler giant I could not have met. Though he was known to me in childhood when he ministered in Glasgow, this did not induce familiarity.

During those formative years when he called in our home I am sure it never once occurred to him that this child would one day feature in God's plan for his care at the end of his earthly pilgrimage. What a weighty thought! Oh! how intricate is the plan of God for our lives; no detail, however small, is overlooked. It takes a lifetime for all the pieces to come together; yet every single one has been planned and designed with each of us in mind before the foundation of the world was laid. I find this a staggering thought, but it is simple to the One of whom Job wrote that, 'He hung the world upon nothing'.

In the course of this patient's hospitalisation I recall one morning undertaking a certain task accompanied by a colleague. The good man made an interesting comment which revealed the channel in which his thoughts were flowing. The skin on the soles of the feet becomes thickened owing to the intermittent pressure of walking. During illness, particularly when bedrest is prolonged, this skin loses its elasticity, becomes dried and eventually flakes off as dead skin. While we attended to his feet, he said, in Gaelic, "Oh! remove as much as you can, it will be a little less of this sinful body which I will require to carry around with me". I never forgot this. A small thought to some but the sentiments are profound.

Many friends, denied the privilege of visiting this saint, used to ask me to convey their good wishes, often accompanied by some text. One such friend saw me as God's messenger for she had been praying for a means of communicating with him just before I was sent to the ward. I certainly did not see myself thus even when, following off duty, he would enquire as to whom I had seen and whether they had 'anything' for him. I knew precisely what he meant. He was looking for a token, a promise, spiritual encouragement. He would often say he wished to recover only to preach the infallible word. One lady I met asked me to convey a promise she had received while she was praying for him. She was thoroughly convinced it meant his recovery and she wished me to make this known. The text was, 'Thy brother shall rise again'. I did as I was bidden, but I was soon to learn, and so was she, that wisdom is required in the interpretation of Scripture; it may have more than one meaning.

Despite this rapport I was often bewildered when on occasions he would say things like, "I wish our *Margaret was like you", meaning his daughter, or when, as happened once as I brought his evening meal into his room, he refused to eat until I had shared in his meal. In deference we always waited until he said grace, but this request was one I did not wish to comply with. I felt embarrassment. Even so, the significance of the request was not entirely lost on me. I somehow knew within myself that it was of a spiritual nature. Without my realising it he was at this time on the very threshold of Glory. Today as I look back I feel very privileged, although at the time his interest mystified. As far as I was concerned I was still in the same spiritual mould. Nothing had changed. I hadn't attained any spiritual excellence. I hadn't attended a prayer meeting or made any profession relative to the state of my soul and so during these weeks I often felt pharisaic, as if I were deceiving this good man of God.

A heavy sleeper, I never used to wake until the bell rang. One morning, shortly after the above event, I awoke around 6.00 a.m. and my thoughts drifted to this patient. It is customary to receive a ward report at the beginning of each shift and so we assembled in the duty room. Each patient is reported on. When the night nurse came to the Reverend gentleman, those of us who were on the previous evening shift were quite shocked to hear her say he had passed away at 6.00 a.m. He seemed so well when we went off duty. Certainly there was no evidence to suggest his sudden demise, at least not to a mere student. I had an overwhelming desire to see his remains, but I recognised the impossibility of this as the undertaker was already in his room. It was, therefore, all the more amazing to hear Sister ask me, as the person nearest to the door, to ensure that a certain task was fulfilled. My desire was granted. I looked on his mortal frame, his soul now forever with his Lord and I gazed in wonder, in longing and with a great deal of sadness. He had cared for my soul; now he was forever gone from the scene of time. To the reader this may seem a strange morbid desire, but I sincerely believe it was the 'perfect desire' to which the Psalmist refers and which, through His Truth, we are assured He will accomplish. I had just passed my eighteenth birthday; perhaps even I never fully understood, but I had no doubt it was from the Lord. 'Until the day break and the shadows flee away'. His passing left an enormous void and now, forty years on, I can look back and think of these few weeks as a great spiritual experience.

Another, never to be forgotten incident, occurred while I was working on the same ward. Commencing duty one morning, an elderly gentleman who had been an in-patient for some time, but was reasonably well, began to exclaim, "Oh! the angels, the angels". On being asked where they were he said, "In the ward and around my bed. Can you not see them?" It seemed incredible to him that we could not perceive the activity around him. The ward domestic, overwhelmed by the occurrence, stopped what she was doing, picked up her brushes and walked out of the ward. Later that day the angels accompanied that man to Glory.

Shortly after this I started attending the weekly prayer meeting and two years later in Glasgow I made public profession of my faith. I still hadn't a sense of definite spiritual experience with which to come to the Lord's Table, but I longed to cast in my lot with the Children of God. I wished to come out completely on His side and make this known to the world. Yet I had no awareness of assurance of salvation. All I had as I walked towards the church hall where the session met was the words of the Psalmist,

> *'One thing I of the Lord desired,*
> *And will seek to obtain,*
> *That all days of my life I may*
> *Within God's house remain'.*

How would the Session address this? Would they let me forward to the Table? or having weighed me in the balance would I be found wanting? These were real anxieties. I went in, saw all these elders and felt numb. The minister asked his opening question in a warm tone. "What brings a young girl like yourself before this Session tonight?" I remember no more, but I did receive my token and Oh! what it meant. It was the most precious piece of metal I had ever handled and if my heart was heavy when I went in, my mourning was turned to gladness. Perhaps I should pause here long enough to explain to the reader what is meant by token. It is a small flat piece of lead bearing the name of the church on one side and the words, 'This do in remembrance of me', on the other. It is given to members the day before the sacrament and handed over to the presiding elder on approach to the Communion Table. It is a means of safeguarding the Table from unbelievers.

Training days were now coming to an end. They had passed as training days do, a lot of hard work, humour and fun, but Africa still remained high on the agenda. My imagination would soar with each overhead aircraft, coming to earth as we landed in Africa. Fashioning the clay had only just begun.

chapter six

Not As I Will

'He shall reign from pole to pole
With illimitable sway'.

On my last holiday home before the conclusion of my training, as was my wont, I frequented my aunt's home across the road, yet, nothing prepared me for the news my younger aunt shared with me on the final day of my leave. It was shortly before the spring communion and when I entered she was very occupied airing bed linen and mattresses. Every bed had two mattresses, one stored under the other. This was the reserve bed for the communions, when visitors were often required to bed down on the floor. Very comfortable, I assure you, and a common practice in households where upwards of twenty people may sleep in any one night. This hive of activity was shared by her elder sister, a spastic, following a birth injury. Together they cleaned, aired, touched up paintwork and baked, in readiness for their influx of visitors.

Amidst all this and out of earshot of her sister, my aunt paused long enough to discuss a few pleasantries and wish me well in my last term of training. Before bidding me goodbye she said, "I have cancer and I will require to see about it after the communions". I was simply floored. Seldom expressed in these days, and certainly not with the cool demeanour of the person who stood beside me in the kitchen, cancer was a dread word. Even more so than it is today. Frequently you would hear of a sufferer as having, 'An aon rud', (the one thing), but never cancer.

It was known that my aunt had a peptic ulcer and I assumed her pain was associated with this. I tried to convince the unconvincable. Her conviction as to her condition was absolute. We said goodbye, I still in disbelief; after all she had not yet seen her doctor! I left for Glasgow, not having shared her news with the family, my own thoughts in confusion. This was a favourite aunt to whom I was close, but she was not just favoured by me but by the body of believers at large. It seemed incongruous that she should suffer from this disease.

The communion weekend over, her great friend the minister's wife called on her way to the mid-week service. My aunt had had a full house during this weekend, but she had carried it through with her secret intact. On this particular evening as she and her friend deliberate over the services and events of the weekend, my aunt recounts the wonderful blessing her soul received at the Lord's Table. As they prepared to leave for the prayer meeting the minister's wife remarked on how well my aunt looked. It was an unusual remark, but one that led to the response, "I am not well at all, I have cancer and I am dying, I have sat at the Lord's Table on earth for the last time". There was no emotion, no self pity, but a sheer matter-of-factness, born out of acceptance of what her Lord had disclosed to her. In amazement, the minister's wife began to remonstrate with her, as I had done the previous week, but to no avail.

After a visit to the outpatient clinic my aunt was subsequently hospitalised for investigation. Her faith held firm and when, following an operative procedure, her minister, with the family's permission, spoke with the Consultant; he advised him to inform my aunt of her diagnosis. This was uncommon in the fifties. Rather was the diagnosis withheld from the patient, supposedly in their best interest. We nurses became adept at fobbing off questions, something which troubled some of us a great deal. It was really quite hard keeping up a facade between patients and their relatives. Often we were aware that patients had already assumed the worst and the roundabout way in which their questions were being answered only confirmed this to them. We felt sad deceiving them, denying them the opportunity to speak frankly when they evidently wished to do so, but it was the professional attitude of these times. Death and dying was not generally an open subject. In any case, as students we did not have the authority to disclose any information. Thankfully the professions are much more enlightened today.

The news of a carcinoma was no surprise to my aunt. She anticipated her Heavenly home. She was ready to meet her Maker. Matthew Henry puts it very succinctly, 'Our being ready for death will never make it come the sooner, but the much easier'. Thus she waited, expecting to be discharged when her wound healed. She was, therefore, the more stunned when the Consultant, stopping by her bedside, apologised as he informed her that the result of her biopsy, just received, was benign. I received a letter from her at this time which read, '... The result of my biopsy is negative. I cannot believe it. I feel only disappointment. God's promise unfulfilled, never! Pray for me as I face surgery, the second time in ten days ...'. Disappointment with the news! I couldn't believe her reaction or fully understand her sentiments. I felt liberated for her. I was then twenty-one years of age and I was certain that if I had received such a result in the same circumstances I would have been delighted. How much I had to learn. She looked beyond herself to the God who said she had cancer and now she felt His honour was at stake. His Glory was all important.

Less than a week after her second laparotomy the pathology report was received. This time the Consultant had offered no information until he was certain of the result. 'Carcinoma of head of pancreas with secondaries in the liver'. Again he visited, again he apologised. He had operated the second time with a view to removing part of her stomach and it was then he found the offending tumour. My aunt was aware that no corrective surgery had been undertaken. She was not a nurse, but she had expected all the paraphenalia of tubes and drips and there were none. Friends bemoaned the needlessness of two exploratory operations, but by grace she remained totally resigned. The path chosen was not of the surgeon's making. His eyes were held. He was only the instrument God used to bring His own plans to fruition. He was testing the faith of His child. She looked on it as His will, part of His sanctifying process. Would she not drink the cup her Father had chosen for her? She felt only relief; His Glory was not put to shame. Had He not said? She looked into the face of the promise. Abba Father.

Two weeks later she was discharged home in the care of a nurse friend who could administer the drug regime prescribed. Six weeks prior to her death, my training complete, I returned home. Sharing in her care was an incredible experience. I was now a registered nurse, but I had never met a patient who talked openly of dying. My aunt was a small producer of Harris Tweed and my first task when we were alone was to bring her the drawers of her bureau. One by one she explored the contents with my help. This must be burned, this could be left, this I could take with me when she was gone, this page and that from her ledgers should be destroyed and so it went on. She advised me of her will. She had given my father instructions regarding her funeral and the money to pay for it. She suggested an appropriate gift from the family to give her friend after her death. I was amazed. There was no pretending, but instead an openness which enhanced her death bed. What a difference it made to the family and friends who saw her. Within three months of her prophetic conversation with both myself and the minister's wife, death heralded her into the presence of her Lord. This experience was to colour my view of death and dying for the remainder of my working life.

It is probably not inappropriate, as a post-script, to include something she left written in a jotter and to which she put her name.

'It is our duty to witness faithfully, to persevere unto the end, to be constantly in prayer for the church's needs and the Lord will see to it that His cause and Kingdom will prevail. Instead of doing damage to the church this may have the effect of awakening her out of the spiritual lethargy that is too evident and perhaps the effect of purifying her as well and the need for that is nonetheless evident. Let us get more occupied pleading the power that will revive souls in truth and bless to that end the labours of the few who toil day and night, often in tears sowing the seed. Let us take courage and toil with them, and then we shall also have cause to rejoice with them and perhaps reap sheaves'.

For a few months after my aunt's death and while I awaited the commencement of my midwifery training, a must for Africa, I worked in the local hospital. The midwifery course was then of a year's duration and part two was almost complete when I had a letter from my mother advising me that my father was unwell and suggesting that I should come home. She went on to say that his illness was of a terminal nature, although the general practitioner had never suggested this. I knew my mother well enough not to question the wisdom of her words. After making the necessary arrangements I went home indefinitely on leave without pay.

My father suffered acute breathlessness of sudden onset. The doctor advised that he had a mass in his left lung and wished to hospitalise him for a series of tests. My mother straightly refused, indicating that it would only increase my father's discomfort unnecessarily. I tried to persuade her but I didn't push the issue, though, as a nurse, I felt embarrassed, in the presence of the doctor, by her decision. But she was right. Within five weeks my father had passed from time into Eternity. How did my mother know my father's illness was terminal?

Early one morning while my father was still in health she had a strange dream which she understood to be verified by a text my father was vocalising as he awoke the same morning. Arising to make tea for them both, he shared with my mother the verse of scripture in his mind. 'Father, I will that they also whom thou hast given me be with me where I am that they may behold my Glory ....'. Their conversation over this text is not known to me, nor my father's conclusions. I do know my mother concluded that my father was soon to be called Home. It should not be thought that a Christian remains untouched by circumstances such as these. Christians are very human, very sensitive, but they plead with their Father for sustaining grace. My mother went about her daily chores and did not share her thoughts with anyone, least of all with the daughter who was away from home.

About a week into my leave my father said to me, "You were at home only six weeks before your aunt's death. It doesn't seem as though you will be home much longer this time". He turned to my mother and said, "this insatiable thirst reminds me of my mother's death". It was his way of communicating what he already knew and it gave us the opportunity to be forthright with him. My mother responded by reminding him of the Home to which he was going, saying, "Oh! how fortunate you are going Home with your Lord. Think of me left behind on my own". Solemnly, he said, "You are not the one facing Eternity and bereft of hope". In complete contrast to my mother's strong faith, my father experienced intense doubt which blighted his spiritual comfort on his death bed. It was the story of his Christian life. He was among those who, 'fear the Lord .... but walk in darkness and have no light'. This occasion was the only time I saw my mother's loneliness surface. Someone once wrote that 'parting is such sweet sorrow'. I'm not sure that it is. There seems little sweetness in parting when overwhelming isolation is being worked through. The Christian clings to the Lord and knows His comfort in these, as in all trying circumstances; but the Christian, in common with others, must pass through the grieving process which, although it may not seem like it at the time, is a healing process.

On the evening to which I refer, as we sat together around the fire, I arose. It was too much for me. Soon, we knew not how soon, our small family would be depleted and it would never be the same again. It was, for me, overwhelming, yet my mother conducted herself with serenity. I never saw her weep, though I am sure she did. With hindsight I handled my mother's bereavement badly. I was not only inexperienced, but I was too locked in my own responses to allow my mother share her grief or encourage her mourning. While I remained at home I kept us both occupied, thinking this was the answer, the way forward; anything to keep us from dwelling on our hurt. Instead of walking the road of grief together and becoming closer through it, in our sorrow we seemed to walk apart, neither wishing to upset the other.

Throughout my father's short illness, my mother had an uncanny knowledge of what was happening. The last evening he was alive, she suggested we should split the night between us. It was our custom to remain with him each night. His breathlessness had improved with drugs and he was up each day, but on the evening in question my mother became anxious that we had not bought black clothes. Black was not then worn except during mourning, as a token of respect. She wished me to go into town next morning to buy something. It was a depressing thought as I was aware that my mother did not expect my father to last long. She arose, as she suggested, and I had only climbed into bed when I heard her call. I was in time to catch my father alive, slumped in my mother's arms. It was a nice way to go. His suspected cancer was not the cause of his death.

It is amazing how quickly guilt assails. This is well recognised as a syndrome of grieving. I soon began to say to myself, why did I not do this or that, say this or not say that? Two weeks after the funeral I returned, heartbroken, to complete my training. Life was in a turmoil. Would I ever see Africa? Could I really leave my mother, who since her sister's death eighteen months previously had the oversight of her spastic sister, even though she resided alone in her family home? With a sore heart I felt I humanly couldn't. Within less than two years this aunt had passed from time into Eternity. There followed a year later news of the death of my mother's only surviving brother in Brazil. Africa receded further.

Three months after my father's death, my course complete, I return to the Island. After working as a midwife for three years I successfully applied for a district post. A short period of training ensued and I spend nine happy years working in the community. It was then suggested to me that I should undertake health visitor training. At that time a pure health visiting service was unknown in these Islands and the local authority agreed to second me. My mother's only surviving sister, herself now alone, consented to stay with my mother. This allowed me to go with an easy mind, as far as my mother was concerned, but many were my apprehensions. Even in these days Health Visiting was a comprehensive course with many subjects, for example, sociology, psychology, etc., new to me. Would I make it? Would I let my employing authority down? With God's help and hard study I did make it. But there were other problems, ones I never even thought of.

One morning, during my Christmas break, as we listened to the radio, my aunt gave a startled exclamation. An East coast fishing vessel was missing around Unst and, yes, the name signified that it was the boat on which her son worked. Soon the telephone rang confirming the news to her. All day we listened to radio reports or for the telephone to ring and next morning my aunt returned to her home. A life jacket had been found, the search was called off, there were no survivors. Five young grandchildren were fatherless. This son was extremely good to his mother; she felt his death very keenly and could not forget the children. In time she returned to Lewis with my mother and this somehow eased her loneliness, but it was never far from her mind. By my next vacation, Easter, she was showing evidence of oesophageal problems, but she did not seek medical advice until six months later, despite encouragement. She was hospitalised in her nearest hospital and I took leave to visit her. Our suspicions were confirmed. She had carcinoma of the oesophagus. Eighteen months later she crossed the Jordan of death. Bereavement had to be worked through once more.

My mother became particularly close to this younger sister during their year together when I was in training. It seemed almost like a bonus before she was taken away. With the same serenity, the same stoicism, my mother, by God's grace, accepted His will. I was conscious, however, that she now felt very alone. Her dependence upon me grew. Africa was definitely off the map. Did God intend? No, not Africa, but He did intend that this persuasion would motivate me towards nursing as a profession. Without such a prompting I would never have entered nursing. 'Thy way is in the sea, and Thy path in the great waters and Thy footsteps are not known'.

I was never ambitious despite the width of training I ultimately undertook. Each move was, I believe, of the Lord. I was gently pushed along as each door opened. Conscious of my inadequate performance at school, the fact that I never failed in an exam bespeaks His care of me. I give Him all the Glory. The one job I always said I would never do was administration. Office work seemed so confining and so boring and such a waste of professionalism in contrast with the clinical work in which I was engaged and which I enjoyed so much. Yet God directed my footsteps and gave me an aptitude for the very thing I sought to avoid. When I look back I see His wisdom and His wonderful provision for me. For more than a decade, on account of my health, I could not have functioned at a clinical level. Management was to become my forte. How meticulous His care?

My first introduction to administration was almost imperceptible as the post carried a small health-visiting caseload. I did not even have to apply for this post; it was offered to me and I felt it was God's leading. The re-organised health service was on the horizon and we nurses were expected to view the obligatory changes as a challenge. Blue band circulars were issued regularly by the Scottish Office in the run up to this integrated approach to health care. These were intended to prepare us for the variation in service. Four executive posts were being created locally and one of these in nursing. I knew I was eligible to apply, but it never once gave me a thought. As nurses we pondered the changes, but none of us could say we really welcomed them, for they were not fully understood by us. The weeks passed and the happenings of 1974 still seemed remote.

One morning in mid 1973 as I drove to work, I was arrested by more than the traffic which halted me at the major road sign. A text suddenly spoke to my mind which I could not understand. 'The elder shall serve the younger'. What on earth could it mean? I was still mulling over it as I climbed the stairs and stepped into my office. I wasn't long in when I was made aware of the fact that the adverts for the top posts had been released. I knew my immediate supervisor was to apply. She had previously informed me of her intent. Suddenly the thought flashed. Surely not! The text couldn't possibly relate to the post. I knew I definitely didn't want this post. The responsibility was too much. I didn't know enough about it. Educationally I was convinced I could never do it. I couldn't even see it as a challenge. I wanted nothing to do with it and I couldn't think of one positive reason why I should go for it. My superior was applying; that was sufficient reason for not proceeding further. But the text left me in a state of confusion. I 'phoned my mother. She was a wonderful mentor in such circumstances and I told her of my plight. She spoke from a mother's heart and discouraged me. I had a perfectly adequate, well paid job, she said. Why should I want to move into a calling which was going to give me a lot of extra work? Why indeed? In honesty I could say I didn't want to. I came off the telephone none the wiser and so I let the matter rest.

A week later my mother contacted me. This was so typical of her. Give her a text, a thought and she pursued it until she was convinced of God's answer. "No matter how I feel," she said in Gaelic, "about this new post, the Lord has made it quite clear to me that you must apply. You are going to get the job, but you are going to meet with many difficulties, yet the Lord has promised that He will be with you", and she quoted 'Be strong and of a good courage, fear not, nor be afraid of them, for the Lord Thy God He it is that doth go with thee, He will not fail thee nor forsake'. A wonderful promise. I came off the telephone stunned. First my text with its clear meaning, then my mother's 'phone call with all she had to say, even going so far as to tell me the post for which I had not yet applied was to be mine. I could do no other than sit down and write for an application form. I felt I could not be disobedient to the Heavenly vision. Yet my arguments with Him were not over; like Moses I was loath on account of, as Scripture puts it, my lack of eloquence and feebleness of speech. Even as I placed those arguments before Him I was afraid to refuse His bidding.

Immediately I set about applying for the post obstacles beset my way. I sought a reference from the Medical Officer of Health to whom I was accountable and he contacted his depute to try and dissuade me. Not content with this he journeyed to Stornoway and counselled me in his depute's office. "Go for the second-in-line post", he advised. I listened to his reasoning and quietly responded, "Doctor, I previously informed you that I was making application after prayerful consideration. I am applying for this post and furthermore I am going to get it". I added, "A reference is immaterial". I was astonished by my own assertiveness and I was concerned by my disclosure. This doctor, as far as I was aware, was an agnostic. His depute was not at that time a Christian. I knew they would observe the outcome with interest. "Lord let not thy promise fail", and even as I prayed thus I was assured He wouldn't. His promises can never fail. My anxieties evaporated. God was in control. It was His doing and it would be wondrous in our eyes. Subdued, the Medical Officer of Health told me I could use his name as a referee, but I must remember he had also promised to provide a reference for my superior. I thanked him, left the office, the first obstacle removed.

It was the beginning of many difficulties. Difficulties necessary to my spiritual refinement. The potter must do with His clay as seemeth

Him good. Marred as a consequence of sin, He must take the clay and fashion it until He can make of it a vessel fit for His use. This is a cardinal difference between the believer and the unbeliever. The unbeliever is never aware of the potter's handling and never attributes problems or turmoils to Satan.

As I sat awaiting my turn to be called, an unknown entity to the interviewing panel, I clearly recall the dark forebodings which enveloped my soul. "Lord", I prayed, "if it be Thy will let this cup pass by me, yet not my will but Thy will be done". It was a strange sensation sitting there, not yet interviewed and so assured that by the end of the day I would be offered the post of Chief Area Nursing Officer. Yet, I was so afraid of what it all entailed. Matthew Henry once wrote 'The eye can see the ocean, but not see over it'. I felt I understood this.

For eighteen years I held this post, until in August 1991, I took early retirement, again, I believe, at His bidding. But that is another story.

chapter seven

Peace Out Of Pain

'Ill that God blesses is our good
And unblest good is ill
All is well that seems most wrong
If it be of His sweet will'

Five years after I took up my post with the Health Board, cancer crept into our family again. My mother had but one niece in this country and she and her husband kept in regular contact, visiting us each year.

It used to amaze me how this highly intelligent and successful young man, with little or no interest in matters spiritual, would so readily agree to participate in family worship. The routine was established the first time they visited our home together. My mother specified that each in turn would read a passage of scripture and offer a prayer. Down we would fall on our knees, unconcerned that none but God could hear what was said.

On the Lord's day they were expected to attend church and at mealtimes to take their turn in offering thanks. I never knew either of them to object or show any resistance, even if our practice did not conform to their way of life. My mother became very fond of this nephew-by- marriage, exhorting him as regards his soul and praying for him when he was out on the high seas.

Educationally very bright, dux of his school and gaining a scholarship to Gordonston, he nevertheless chose his livelihood from the depths of the sea. No persuasion by his mother could prevail upon him. The call of the sea coursed through his veins drawing him like a magnet to the familial occupation of generations.

Away from home throughout the week, he devoted his weekends to his wife and family and the pleasures associated therewith. Their increasing family were placing constraints on their two bedroom bungalow and so they took the decision to erect a larger and more opulent home. Land was procured and construction commenced. Previous to this, his wife had launched their new boat, which was now at sea and very successful. He worked hard for his family, wishing to secure for them a lifestyle of comfort and one commensurate with his own status. Into this situation God spoke.

It was a weekend and Kenneth was home from sea. Standing at the kitchen window he suddenly complained of acute abdominal pain. Gradually receding, he was able to return to work at the appropriate time. It was, however, but the beginning of several such episodes which culminated in a visit to his doctor. Overweight, he was told this was the root of his problem and advised to diet. Still the pain persisted, necessitating several visits to the health centre. With weight loss and jaundice now in evidence, he was sent for 'straight' X-rays which revealed no abnormality. His wife worried deeply and so did we for them.

On his last trip to sea before the boat tied up for the Christmas break, he felt very unwell. When he came ashore his wife urged him to seek a second opinion and finally, requesting private consultation, he was admitted to hospital. With no one to turn to Joan would 'phone her family in Lewis and try and explore what our opinion of his condition was. We were obviously very anxious for his symptoms did not augur well. My mother at this time was much exercised about his soul while her concern for her young niece, with her heavy responsibilities, often spilled over. Apart from prayer it was difficult to broach the subject from any other angle, particularly as the Minch separated us.

Kenneth's visit to hospital co-incided with the removal to their new home. His wife had to effect this move, while at the same time driving the one hundred and twenty mile return journey to hospital each day. She spoke frequently with medical personnel, to be told that her husband was receiving tests and results were awaited. She was never given any indication as to his suspected condition. It was, therefore, all the more surprising to hear her husband's voice on the telephone one morning, advising her of the news which he had just received. Ten days after admission his Consultant discharged him home giving him the full facts of his diagnosis. "Mr. Wood, I understand you are a business man with a young family. I am sure you will want to put your affairs in order and I am not going to beat about the bush. You have two tumours, in bowel and liver, both of which are inoperable. I would say you have about four weeks to live". Devastating news by anyone's standards, but to his young wife who stood by the telephone as he gave her this news, it was positively shattering. Meantime, in the nurse's home a second year enrolled nurse student was being challenged to go down to the ward and pray with 'Mr. Wood'. Off duty, he was unaware of the Consultant's news. He reasoned with his Lord, how could he go down and pray?, after all he was a student, he was off duty and nurses were not in the habit of praying with their patients. But down he did go. "Mr. Wood, would you like me to have a word of prayer with you?" Devastated by the tidings he had just received he acknowledged the nurse's gesture with a mere "if you want to". The nurse did.

That night as we spoke with them both by telephone, while Joan was completely broken, Kenneth was quite composed as he told us exactly what the Consultant had said. Then, aware that we would be pleased, he spoke of the young male nurse who prayed with him, adding, "if it were not for that nurse I might have been a very bitter man tonight". I never forgot this, for it was a very interesting comment from one who was not, at that time, converted.

In the background, my mother laboured for the salvation of his soul and for sustaining grace for her niece who had three children, a baby of three months, a child of two and a child of four years, to care for. It was a really poignant time for all concerned. But into this domestic turmoil stepped the Lord.

The male student to whom reference has already been made requested the opportunity to visit Kenneth in his home. At the same time the skipper of a sister vessel, himself recently converted, called to see his friend. Both young men wrestled with God on his behalf; they exhorted him to pray and showed him the way of salvation through Christ Jesus. As they persisted in their endeavours, God's light eventually broke through the darkness that surrounded Kenneth's soul. The effect was tremendous. He had absolutely no doubt as to what God had effected in him and he immediately began to tell his family and friends what great things God had done. A telephone call away, we soon rejoiced with them. Momentarily the sadness receded. It was as if an ethereal light broke through the chilly cloud which enveloped us all. I wrote him at this time and enclosed Mrs. Cousin's poem on Samuel Rutherford's last words, "In Immanuel's Land', or perhaps as it is better known,

> 'The sands of time are sinking
> The dawn of heaven breaks'.

These words spoke such sweet joy to his soul that he requested their reading at his funeral, together with the singing of the hymn,

> 'Will your anchor hold
> In the streams of life'.

I am sure this latter was chosen with his sea-faring friends in mind.

Another favourite passage was John Chapter 14 Verse 2. His friend Joe introduced him to John's gospel when he first called to see him. After his conversion Kenneth could be heard to repeat with great fervency, 'In my Father's house are many mansions: if it were not so I would have told you. I go to prepare a place for you'.

What a transformation! While he was able he couldn't stop talking of what God had done for his soul, even advising his four year old son that Jesus was coming soon to take him to Heaven with Himself. It was incredible. But Satan did not leave him for long. He came in the guise of an angel of light, probably the most difficult form in which to recognise him.

A well-meaning friend called, who obviously believed in baptismal regeneration, and during their discussion the issue of baptism was raised. The view was expressed that baptism was essential to salvation. This began to trouble Kenneth a great deal and his friend offered to administer baptism by immersion in the domestic bath. Joan felt he was too ill for this and in any case she was of the opinion that if what was being suggested was true, her aunt would have advised them. A 'phone call ensued and my mother tried to outline the biblical interpretation for the administration of this sacrament. The issue obviously continued to distress Kenneth as it was the first thing he sought clarification on when I went out to see him. I tried to explain the matter as simply as I could and as he was very tired I concluded by assuring him that there were many in hell who had been baptised and many in heaven who were never baptised. Baptism was not essential to salvation. This seemed to give him great ease of mind for he never spoke of it again.

That evening we had worship together in the sitting room, Kenneth read and prayed and then returned to bed. Next morning he was too tired even to read and suggested we should conduct worship ourselves. This we did by his bedside. Two days later and four weeks after his diagnosis, the Lord called him Home, there to gaze in wonder on the face of his Redeemer. He was but on loan to his family, the loan was now up. It could be said of him that he was 'a brand plucked from the burning'.

During the brief period I was with them it was evident that he was too ill to absorb the mental anguish through which his wife was passing. He had already committed the family to the care of the All Knowing One. I saw him make a super-human effort to kiss his sons, quite without my realising it was his goodbye. Many times in the few weeks Kenneth was home, Joan, her heart torn with grief, would say, "What will I do without you?", and he would wisely advise on how she should fulfill her life. It was almost as if they were working out their grief together. At all times he appeared resigned to his early home call.

When I made an abortive attempt to visit them, the 'plane unable to land in the snow, Kenneth said to his wife that perhaps the Lord had withheld me until a more appropriate time. This certainly appeared so. I think he knew he was almost within the fold and he expected the Lord to send me before the end.

His spiritual growth in the four short weeks of his Christian life was evident. To his friends he would say "I have lived thirty years on earth, a longer span than many have enjoyed". He knew his friends viewed his early death almost as a waste. He would fain woo them for Christ and for a short while after his death, some were sufficiently concerned to attend church, but gradually the effect wore off. I am sure these words sum up his desire:

'O Lord that I could waste myself for others,
With no ends of my own,
That I could pour myself into my brothers
And live for them alone'.

Emotion is not enough, a Spirit wrought work is essential. As his friends slipped back into the world, this was all too evident. Yet we hope that someone, someday may remember and that the remembrance will lead them in repentance to the Lord.

Through conversation by telephone and during the few days I was with him in his home, Kenneth reminisced over what, with hindsight, could be seen as God's preparatory work in his soul. He was a freemason of short duration for his curiosity compelled him to join. I gave him, during his holiday in Lewis, a small Christian booklet which I had purchased on this subject. He confessed that he read therein the very first text which arrested his thoughts. I found this quite interesting, even though there had been no lasting effect. Sometime afterwards the skipper referred to earlier began to discuss his conversion with Kenneth over the ship's radio, as they fished together off the Norwegian coast. In doing so he tried to bring before Kenneth his own lost state. Kenneth would blithely repeat something he heard my mother say and so the conversation went on until Kenneth's illness took over.

Most amazing of all were his thoughts the morning the Consultant advised him of his condition. As Kenneth awaited the ward round he was thinking, "All I need now is the health to work to pay off my new boat and the mortgage on the house". He was hoping the doctors were going to advise him of what they proposed doing. Through his mind flashed a Bible story which he assumed he must have heard in Sunday School years before. It was about the rich man who knocked down his barns and built bigger ones and to whom the Lord addressed the words, 'thou fool, this night thy soul shall be desired of thee'. It is remarkable the ways in which the Lord breaks up the fallow ground to receive the seed.

When they were born I gave each of the children a New Testament, together with a present. In the fly leaf of the Testament I gave their infant son I had written the inscription, 'As thy days so shall thy strength be'. This came to me as I was about to ask my mother if she could think of an appropriate text of Scripture. Kenneth remarked on this text in these last days, announcing that "these words were for me". Yes, they were for him. In his illness the strength of the Lord was indeed commensurate with his days. He is now asleep in Jesus, but when he 'shall awake he will be satisfied with His likeness'. His dust, which lies in the grave, is united to Christ until the Resurrection. What a thought! We who are dust returning to dust and that dust, in the case of the believer, united to Christ who inhabits Eternity. What mystery! Blessed day when we too join the heavenly throng and we see Him as He is.

chapter eight

An Island Blessed

'Look down from heaven and behold and visit this vine'

Following on from Kenneth's illness, I was the next member of our now small family to present with cancer. This occurred six months after Kenneth's death. It was, in fact, this personal encounter with the disease which motivated close friends to encourage me to record my experience, something I have, over many years, resisted.

It is June 1979 and the special services are being conducted in the Free Church in Stornoway. The Tuesday evening service is led by one of the church's senior ministers and, in common with many others, I make my way there. These special services are held once a year for four to five consecutive evenings in each congregation. With the exception of Stornoway, the season of choice is November through to January. Instituted as evangelical services and directed towards the spiritual needs of the unconverted, in my youth they were well attended. Sadly, in recent years there has been a gradual decline in the numbers of unconverted persons attending.

Readers unfamiliar with our Island are bound to wonder at the religious tenor of our way of life and this might not be an inappropriate juncture at which to pause and share a little of the workings of God's spirit in our midst.

An account of the Island in the mid-eighteenth century gives reason to believe that there was a spiritual dearth prevailing. Available documentation reveals that the few resident ministers were of moderate persuasion and in some cases doubt is cast on their personal interest in salvation. More concerned about their stipend, which far exceeded that of the tradesmen of their day, and the acreage of their glebes, they expressed little or no anxiety for the souls of the people. Interestingly, the Lord's Supper was celebrated and everyone over a given age was permitted to participate.

A druidical temple, familiarly known as the standing stones, and the largest after Stonehenge, gives evidence of pagan rites, while the ruins of convents marks the dominance of Roman Catholicism. It is into this spiritual vacuum, exactly one hundred and seventy years ago, a Godly minister is settled. The people turn out to hear what he has to say and after a relatively brief period a quickening interest is observed. The minister initiates mid-week prayer meetings in different parts of the district where he labours and, little by little, spiritual understanding is awakened. The people, some in deep concern, realise their lost condition and turn away from their sins.

When the minister arrived in their midst he suspended the communion services, fearing the people could not discern what they were doing. These were now re-established and on the first occasion only nine persons came forward to partake of the Lord's supper. The attendances at the services increased, the spirit fell with power upon the people and by the year 1828, the whole Island appeared to be moved in powerful revival. An estimated nine thousand are said to have assembled at the Lord's Table that year. Week by week souls were being quickened.

The light that rose in Lewis in 1824 still shines today. In the intervening years the tide of the spiritual life of the people has ebbed and flowed with pockets of revival sweeping over certain areas from time to time. None, perhaps, in recent times, was quite so outstanding as the Carloway revival of 1934. It was remarkable in the evidencing of Gospel power and striking in the remarkable understanding ordinary folk had of the word of God. Large groups met regularly for fellowship, prayer and the sharing of spiritual experiences. I remember quite a number of these great stalwarts of the faith and learned much through association with them. They loved the lambs of the flock and Oh!, how this was reciprocated! It is always a healthy characteristic when the lambs desire to follow and feed with the sheep. We loved to frequent the company of these pious men and women and the spiritual atmosphere at times was redolent of heaven.

In subsequent years there have been minor revivals in various parts of the Island, each leaving its own mark, but none quite so spectacular as the one to which reference has been made. I will always appreciate the fellowship of these remarkable converts of the thirties, many of them now in Glory but some still prominent in our midst.

This Island has been singularly blessed and that over many years. It continues to enjoy spiritual privileges today, not known in measure elsewhere, at least that I am aware of. There is no lack of criticism, by one medium or another, of our narrowness of life, of our Calvinistic rigidness and even of our peculiarism, yet our way of life seeks to fulfil but what is expected of the Christian in the word of God. 'If ye will obey my voice ... keep my covenant, then ye shall be a **peculiar** treasure unto me above all people', '.... and the Lord hath chosen thee to be a **peculiar** people unto Himself ... For the Lord hath chosen Israel for His **peculiar** treasure', and in the New Testament we read '.... and purify unto Himself a **peculiar** people' and again 'Ye are ... a **peculiar** people ...'. Matthew outlines that 'narrow is the way'. Thus abundant evidence manifests that there must indeed be a difference between the world and the people of God. Unfortunately, Christians today are embarrassed by what scripture expects of them and they make efforts to conform to the ways of the world. This is the difference noted in Lewis. There are within its shores a spiritual people prepared to be seen as different and whatever is levelled against them, heightens their awareness of the light of God shining in their midst and of devotion to rich experiential Christianity. We deny not a difference, thankful that the wonderful doctrines of the Word of God continue to be expounded freely and in purity.

As I write I long that the young in our midst may continue to cherish the rich heritage that is ours and bear the same remarkable fruits that their forebears bore and which set them apart as a people of God for several generations. What we enjoy we must labour to keep, otherwise the Lord may alter His candle, as He has done in other places throughout the world.

Is change, therefore, in evidence? I think it is. The infiltration of modern thinking, the outstanding media developments and the growth of materialism is having an impact on believers in Lewis as elsewhere. Faced with the many and different hosannahs sung there is grave danger that our youth will succumb or indeed that some may already have done so, thus we need fresh outpourings of His Spirit to awaken our people, for we seem to have entered Bunyan's Land of enchantment. I hope there will never be a return to pagan days or worse, but there is evidence of this having occurred in areas equally as blessed as ours is today. Let us take heed.

Having voiced this concern, I delight that in our midst, lives continue to be touched in remarkable ways. We enjoy something very special, very precious and quite distinctive and yet we long to behold the beauty of holiness clothing our people, myself included, as we once did. Yes, He beheld from heaven, and He visited this His vine, over and over again. A privileged people, much will be required of us.

But what of the 'vine' He visited on that evening in 1979? I sat under the preaching of the Word, enthralled by the way that venerable preacher expounded it, little realising that before the conclusion of the day my world would have turned upside down. When He commands there is no evading His order, the matter is settled and we cannot alter a jot or a title.

As I drove home my mind wandered to the retirement presentation with which I was to be involved the following Friday. I always prefaced my plans with "God Willing", but I still expected to be there! Did I pause to consider that perhaps God had planned something different for me? Sadly not, this encounter with Him was entirely unexpected. But we cannot refuse His summon. In a split second my pleasant musings gave way to a heavy, weary mental exercise. He had visited His vine, not as I would, but as He ordained. Bless His Name He did.

'A Father's hand will never cause
His child a needless tear'.

chapter nine

Darkness Falls

'*Our life is as water spilt on the ground
which cannot be gathered again*'.

When I was on district I came across the following lines, which I think worthy of inclusion in their entirety for they have meant so much to me over the years. I have no idea where they came from or who wrote them, but I do know how heartily I responded to the opening words, for had I not prayed that I might be made like my saviour, that I might have a passion for souls and that I might be found leaning upon Himself. How often we Christians pray thus, entirely sincere in our longings, but with little thought as to the means He may employ in their fulfilment.

'*She asked to be made like her Saviour,
And He took her at her word,
And sent her a heart crushing burden
Till the depths of her soul were stirred.
She asked for a faith strong but simple
He permitted the dark clouds to come,
She staggered by Faith through the darkness
As the storms did her soul overwhelm.*

She prayed to be filled with a passion
 Of Love for lost souls and for God,
And again in response to her longing
 She sank 'neath the chastening load.
She wanted a place in his Vineyard
 And He took her away from her home,
And placed her among hardened sinners
 Where she humanly stood all alone.

She gave up all wordly ambition
 Those "castles in air" of years,
And she knelt in deep consecration
 And whispered 'AMEN' through her tears.
She wanted a meek lowly spirit
 And the work He gave answered that cry,
And those that had been her companions
 With pitying smile passed her by.

She asked to lean hard on her Saviour,
 He took human props quite away,
Till no earthly friend could help her
 And she could do nothing but pray.
I saw her go out of the Vineyard
 To harvest the golden grain,
Her eyes were still moistened with weeping
 Her heart was still throbbing with pain.

But many a heart that was broken
 And many a wrecked blighted life
Was made to thank God for her coming
 And rejoice in the midst of strife.
She had prayed to be made like her Saviour
 And the burden He gave her to bear
Had been but the great Sculptor's training
 Thus answering her earnest prayer.'

We need to be reminded that He it is who gives the burden, He who permits the dark seasons and He who is the Sculptor. The troubles and cares and sickness, resulting from sin and the lot of mankind, is often used by Him, the faithful Burden-Bearer, as a means to sanctify His own children. It is a process necessary before they can see His face. The most amazing fact is that these experiences can produce such surprising and unexpected delight. Why?, because faith in Him is wrought out in these manifestations. This is what I was about to learn.

On that eventful evening as I retired to bed, thinking, as I was, sleepy negative thoughts, I was suddenly aware of a lump I had not noticed before. By every means known to me I examined it, but it remained a small menacing, clearly defined growth. Was it malignant or benign? I couldn't tell. I was very aware of the possibilities and by extra-sensory perception or some such sensation within my being, I was sure it was. Yet, I did not allow myself to dwell on it too deeply. I had nothing from my Lord by way of a confirmatory response through His Truth. I tried, therefore, to be sensible about it, at least until I knew something more positive. I would seek medical opinion, God willing, in the morning.

It was now midnight. With bleakness of soul and with darkness enveloping my life, sleep was difficult. Each time I awoke I examined my discovery. Each time it was there, no bigger, no smaller, but a certainty. Amazingly, I have no recollection of spiritual thought, of prayer or of the word of God dealing with me. It was just a numb unreal feeling. I know I must have called on my Lord, for it would be normal for me to do so in such circumstances and I probably turned it all over to Him, as would be my wont, but I can recall nothing.

> *'Leave God to order all thy ways*
> *And hope in Him whate'er betide*
> *Thou'lt find Him, in the evil days*
> *Thine all sufficient strength and guide*
> *Who trusts in God's unchanging love*
> *Builds on the rock that nought can move!'*

This lovely stanza was written by a George Newark in the seventeenth century. It is told that the words 'Who trusts in God's unchanging love' lay like a burden on his heart. He kept going over and over and over it in his mind until the words formed themselves into a song. He could never tell how, but he began to sing and to pray for joy and to bless God and word followed word.

Although I was at that time engulfed in darkness and a deeper darkness was to follow, yet I too was to sing my song. Joy, as the sweet Psalmist wrote, was to come in the morning, but it wasn't to be the next or the next morning. I had to learn to allow God to teach me how He would order aright my life and conversation. I was to learn to hope in Him as I never had before, to trust Him - my all sufficiency.

Morning dawns at last. I breakfast but mention nothing to my mother. No point in worrying her unnecessarily until I really have to. At work I try to leave everything as orderly as I can, knowing that I will require to enter hospital for at least a biopsy. It is Wednesday morning and I expect to be involved in interviews the following Monday. My secretary is to terminate her post on Friday. I must buy her a present and arrange for someone to give it to her. I glance through the window, allowing myself to absorb the magnificent view before me. There is the inner harbour through which the passenger ferry will shortly sail, to unload her travelling public at the pier; there are the beautiful wooded Castle grounds clothed in hues of the most magnificent purple, the result of masses of rhododendroms. Had anything really changed? Life seemed to go on as before; this was evident from the movement of people and cars on the street below and the everyday routine of the office. Creation remained as inspiring and beautiful as ever. The senses of the mind responded to the excellence of the Creator in His work of creation. What then was so different on this lovely summer's morning? Why suddenly did normality disturb? Why did it seem strange that things went on as before? Why?, because a small round lump no bigger than the nail of my thumb had thrown my life and my thoughts into confusion. What little people we really are! Where was the Lord in all this? Actually, He was developing my need of Him, although I could not see this at the time.

A pre-arranged visit to the surgical clinic is now over. The Consultant sounds cautiously hopeful that the growth is benign, but a biopsy is necessary to confirm diagnosis. Could I come into hospital next morning? Arrangements are made. During this time of consultation I am conscious of the importance of conducting myself as a Christian. I have always held the belief that as in health, so in sickness, a Christian should behave differently from the world. After all, abundant resources are available in Him and we are read of all men. A few weeks previously I had heard disparaging remarks about the manner in which a certain Christian had conducted himself in ill-health. This confirmed to me the need to witness in times of adversity and to bring to God alone the confusion of the heart.

That evening I shared my news with my mother, putting it to her with a light-heartedness I did not feel. In fact I found it very difficult to share my burden with her. I was probably conscious of her vulnerability and of her anxious thoughts for me, her only daughter. In her mid-seventies at the time, I felt she was so unsupported, humanly speaking, and I wanted to shield her. This concern created within me an attitude which probably prohibited her from asking any questions. Yet, I was in no doubt as to where she would take her burden and with whom she would share her anguish. This made her hurt somewhat easier to bear. How different my responses were to be when I actually knew the result.

I contacted a friend in the village with whom I was close, yet, despite her own experiences, we spoke little of the possibilities. We merely acknowledged that God knew what He was doing and where He led we must follow. The awkwardness brought into the lives of friends and close relatives when there is any possibility of cancer is itself interesting. There seems to be a disinclination to face reality or to help another face it. Incredible as it may seem, we would rather weave a web of make-believe than encourage the concerned to face adverse outcomes or discuss fears. My learning curve had just started.

The visit to hospital was brief. I woke up from my anaesthetic declaring that, 'He doth all things well', whatever the ultimate result it would be well. The Consultant reassured me, as much as it was humanly possible to do so at this stage, and informed me he had performed a lumpectomy. The next day I was discharged home and the day following my general practitioner called. He expressed confidence that the lump was benign, but my innate feeling never changed. I smiled, but offered no response. We had coffee and talked platitudes.

Despite my job and the uniqueness of an Island setting, very few people were, at this stage, aware that anything was amiss. The friend to whom I referred called, but other than that I saw no one nor did I speak with anyone by telephone. I returned to work on Monday and conducted the expected interviews. An appointment was made and I attended to the paperwork connected therewith. I found it awkward using my right arm, but I got through the day, with well-meaning colleagues, now aware of my brief stay in hospital, assuring me all would be well. I responded with a simple, "we shall wait and see". The realisation that the result, expected soon, would not be simple was taking root. What then?

During this time my thoughts were frequently with my friend, Morag. I wondered how she felt when she was confronted, eighteen months previously with the same problem. It was something we never thought to discuss. Now I pondered over the heart-searching which must have been her experience. How, I wondered, could she have held the knowledge for three months before she finally sought medical opinion? I felt I could not have done so, but then I did not have three young children to consider.

On the night when I missed her from the service and I rang to enquire if all was well, it was a very listless voice which responded, "Can you come out and see me?". As I reversed the car from the garage, I pondered over our brief conversation. I knew there was something far wrong, but I was mystified as to what it could be.

When I arrived the children were in bed and Morag and her husband were sitting before an inviting peat fire. I was immediately conscious of a heavy heartedness as I quietly enquired as to what was wrong. "I have a lump in my breast", she said. I was lost for words. Was it possible that a nurse, a friend and a sister in the Lord could not find words appropriate to the situation, to the state of mind of these two good friends? How could I lessen their anxiety? I felt such a poor comforter. I knew where their strength lay in time of sorrow and I felt I should be offering some comfort based on this, but as a friend, their thorn pricked me and their pain became my pain. I voiced a few bland, hopelessly inadequate, commonplace sentences. I felt my role was to discourage Morag from dwelling too much on the possibilities. From her attitude and the little she said, I knew she was of the opinion it was malignant. She too was a nurse, but that word malignant was not mentioned by either of us. It seemed an unkindness to air it. It might be this or that, I suggested, everything but what it really was.

I know now what I should have said and done and it would have given Morag the opportunity she probably sought after. Why could I not grasp this situation? Because of what it was doing to me. I couldn't handle my own reactions. I thought, if this was me how would I feel, how would I respond? This application of circumstances and assessment of responses is not uncommon among females and though temporarily stifling, it can produce within the Christian quite positive results.

But why did Morag wait three months before approaching a doctor? She wanted her children to have a happy time at the end of the year without the shadow of her impending ill-health. She exercised a self-denying spirit for the sake of her children. Did this delay exacerbate her condition? In responding to questions such as these, we must never lose sight of the One who plans every minute detail of our lives and who knows exactly what He is doing.

Morag required a mastectomy and follow-up radiotherapy after which she enjoyed a period of two years of relatively good health. During this time and the three years of broken health which were to follow, she devoted herself to her children, instructing them in practical self-sufficiency and in Christian principles, thus preparing them for the time when she would no longer be with them. I remember her telling me after the result of her pathology was made known to her that all she wanted was a little while longer with her children to see them through their tender years. This is a very human and understandable reaction. Two years later, she was to share with me how, on taking a walk in the moor at the back of their home, she sat on a stone and as she gazed around her, God spoke to her through His word and she knew she was not going to recover. "I thought", she said, "that it was necessary for me to be around for the sake of my children, but God made it clear to me He could care for them better than I could myself".

That first night when I learned of Morag's illness, I returned home shattered. I couldn't take in what was happening in her life. I had a deep-seated feeling that her unexpressed fears would be realised. My mother's silence, as I shared Morag's dilemma, spoke volumes, but we did come to discuss it openly together, something which did not happen when I found myself in the same situation. Morag was less than two years my senior, but she and my mother shared a wonderful spiritual rapport which was to grow when they were both ill at the same time. Age is relative; it means nothing in the life of grace.

Eighteen months into the disease which God had programmed for her life, I wondered what she thought when she learned I was about to set out on the same path. There would be similarities, but God deals with us, as He does with all His creatures, as individuals with widely differing personalities.

'*Abide with me; fast falls the eventide*
The darkness deepens; Lord with me abide;
When other helpers fail, and comforts flee
Help of the helpless, O abide with me'.

It is told that the author of these beautiful words was a Scot by the name of Henry Francis Lyte. Born in the eighteenth century, a gifted poet as well as a minister, most of his life he suffered from a persistent strain of tuberculosis. Despite this, he pastored in Devon for twenty four years and it is during this time that it is thought he wrote this hymn. The famous Nurse Edith Cavell is said to have received solace from these words as she faced the firing party in Belguim in 1916, and I am sure that many a Christian over the years, facing their own particular trials, could say the same. The two nurses referred to in this chapter certainly could. As darkness deepened I cried to the Lord for His abiding help, if not in the words of the hymn, certainly in the sentiments they express.

chapter ten

Songs In The Night

---

*'The dark seasons afford the sweetest and strongest manifestations
of the power of faith'.*

When I returned from work that Monday evening, I tried to help
my mother in the preparation of an evening meal for the men who were
assisting us with our peat-cutting activities. Normally I would have
been one of the party, but providence ruled otherwise on this occasion.
It was late in the year, but neighbours required to cut their own and so
we waited until their help was available to us. In a good summer this
did not affect the drying process and we would still have our peats
home in seasonable time. In the middle of this normal domestic scene
my mother called to me, "The doctor's car is at the gate".

As I opened the door and welcomed my general practitioner and the
local consultant surgeon, I immediately knew that they had not arrived
at my home at 6.45 p.m. to give me a benign result. My heart catapulted.
What was the sum of their news? I silently prayed for sustaining grace
and courage. Outwardly remaining placid and in control I took them
into the sitting room and invited them to sit down. My own doctor
spoke first, "I'm sorry, my dear", he said, "but the results indicate that
you have an intra-duct carcinoma which is showing invasive changes".
I questioned them both in some detail and asked if, since I had already
had a lumpectomy, radiotherapy treatment would be sufficient? The

consultant indicated that his preferred option would be mastectomy, pointing out that I might not require radiotherapy at this stage. That would depend on my pathology report and the radiologist's opinion. I felt I should be guided by their decision. They spoke in a practical, but not unsympathetic manner and I had, and still have, great respect for the naturalness and the detail with which I was informed. I responded quite positively about the results being part of God's plan for my life, adding that I wished to leave myself in His care. Establishing that a cup of coffee would be welcome, I temporarily left the room.

When I came out I found my mother anxiously pacing the floor of the small sitting room. "I am going to make some coffee", I informed her, hastily adding, "I have to go into hospital to have my breast removed". She would not have understood the term mastectomy. It was not used in her day and in any case we spoke in Gaelic and there was no Gaelic equivalent. I did not wait to hear her response, but hastened to the kitchen and busied myself with the practicalities of coffee-making.

Following grace and over coffee, we discussed admission. The consultant was anxious that I should go into hospital the following day as Wednesday was a routine theatre day. That agreed, we then conversed over matters of mutual interest in the Health Service. I never felt any emotion, but even if I had, it would have been carefully concealed. There is a time and place for everything. As they took their leave, how little we realised that my general practitioner would, in a few short years, have contracted the same disease and would have passed from the scene of time, while I was left, many years later, to write this story. 'His ways are past finding out'.

When I entered the room where my mother was sitting quietly by the fire, she raised her head and looked silently towards me, waiting to take her cue from whatever I may say. With ponderous and heavy heart I took a seat beside her. As a consequence of our circumstances our thoughts, on this particular evening, were introspective. Facing the situation I thought, there is now no dubiety, I have cancer and cancer is synonymous with death. My thoughts raced on. Is there lymphatic involvement? In layman's terms, am I 'far through'? Do I have long to live? Death! It is inescapable. I find I don't want to die. Why? I know the answer before I ask the question. All my life I have lacked assurance and as a consequence I have been subject to bondage through fear of death. There have, I am ashamed to admit, been occasions when I avoided passages of scripture such as 1st Cor. Ch. 15 or 1st Thess. Ch. 4 vv 13 to the end, because their reference produced anxiety rather than solace. As I waited for light which would illuminate my understanding and dispel my doubts, Satan seemed intent on reminding me, once again, that I couldn't possibly be converted because I had never known a conversion experience, although I could say, 'Entreat me not to leave thee, or to return from following after thee'. With death now a stark reality - it was just as if I was face to face with it - I felt cornered, I desperately wanted to know whether I was born again.

During this time I spoke little. My thoughts were so uptaken with the confirmation of my disease and the plight of my soul that my mother's concerns featured but briefly. This was so different from the week before when I was so anxious for her. I could now only think of myself and my Eternal destiny. It was not the cancer that concerned me, it was Eternity. As I shared a few of these thoughts with her, she encouraged me in the Lord, but I remained as doubtful as to my salvation as Thomas was about the risen Lord. In the middle of our conversation the 'phone rang and I calmly answered it. A friend from another part of the Island was on the line. I shared my news with her. She was quite stunned and her reaction filtered through to me. As soon as appropriate we terminated our conversation.

My mother and I resumed our discussion. On hearing a car stop at our gate my mother glanced through the window and said, "Comfort is at hand, the minister is coming!" I was amazed. Strange, I thought, that he should call at this particular time. I was certain he could not know of our situation, because we had not informed anyone, except the friend who had telephoned. But he did know. Concerned, and aware that we were alone, my friend had thoughtfully 'phoned the Manse.

I do not know how ministers feel when they are confronted with situations such as these, but I am sure it must not be easy for them. I have no doubt the Lord, in preparing them for the office they hold, endows them with a sensitivity towards the needs of the flock in their care. Otherwise, they could not 'rejoice with them that do rejoice and weep with them that weep'; nor could they comfort the sick, the dying, the bereaved and those with sundry difficulties?

On the evening referred to, after a few preliminaries, my mother shared with our minister the fact that I was to be hospitalised on the morrow. Coming from ourselves, I'm sure this information made it easier for him to talk with us. He spoke on the verse, 'There hath no temptation taken you, but such as is common to man, but God is faithful who will not suffer you to be tempted above that ye are able, but will with the temptation also make a way of escape, that ye may be able to bear it'. It was very appropriate to us both, for in the circumstances we both suffered in different ways. While his discussion did not eradicate my train of thought, it certainly gave some relief, for I remember feeling at ease while he expounded these words. Offering prayer he took his leave of us and we both felt thankful to the Lord for His watchful care over us. I did not thereafter revert to my spiritual self-examination until I was alone in my bedroom.

We had an early night. I am sure the tired and weary feelings were mutual, but I was anxious to be alone to think, to reason and to try and find what I felt was missing from my life. My goal was to know that dying meant being with Jesus. Not once did I think of hospital or of having a mastectomy. My soul conflict was too intense to permit even expressed emotion. My whole being was consumed by the need to know where I stood spiritually.

As I write I relive the unforgettable experience of that night. I reasoned over the evidence of grace in my heart or the lack of it. I couldn't say I had a deep sense of conviction of sin, yet I sought to find peace through confessing known sins, forgotten past sins and original sin. But nothing happened. I sought a spirit of repentance. But nothing happened. I sought to discover whether Christ had died for me personally. But I couldn't. I tried to 'believe in the Lord Jesus Christ'. But I couldn't. It was extraordinarily difficult. My soul was fenced in by my troubles. I couldn't appropriate one promise. I held tryst with the Lord and in anguish I begged for mercy. But nothing happened. I tossed and I prayed and I turned and I prayed. But nothing happened. It was as if I was praying into a vacuum. The heavens were truly brass. I decided God was not listening, was not with me in my plight and yet I could not give up praying.

As the night wore on my anguish increased. Then I remembered Hezekiah's prayer when he was told, 'Set thine house in order for thou shalt surely die and not live'. He turned his face to the wall and wept sore. He prayed, and what a prayer, 'O Lord, remember now how I have walked before Thee in truth and with a perfect heart and have done that which is good in Thy sight'. who but Hezekiah could pray thus? Certainly not me. My spiritual life, even in the midst of my zeal, was so sterile and my sins so many. I pondered over what God said to Hezekiah and I thought, "What encouragement". 'I have heard thy prayers, I have seen thy tears, behold I will heal thee ... I will add to thy life fifteen years', the only account in the Bible of additional years being granted to anyone! Fifteen years! it seemed at that moment like another lifetime. Would I like fifteen years added to my life? I thought not. I was afraid I would misuse them and perhaps bring His cause into disrepute. I felt I would prefer what He had willed for me

Despite the change in my thought process I was not comforted. I could have said with Jeremiah, 'He hath hedged me about, that I cannot get out. He hath made my chain heavy and when I cry and shout He shutteth out my prayer', but those words did not come before my mind. Had they, I would have been comforted to know that my case was recorded in God's Book.

Exhausted, I said to myself, "What if I am cast off and I open my eyes in a lost Eternity?". Strangely, I felt no panic at the thought. I reasoned that if I was cast into hell I would be receiving my just reward. I knew God would do with me only what was right in His sight. He could not do otherwise. I had sinned against Him, I deserved Eternal damnation. He would be just in casting me off. Resigned thus to His will, as far as my Eternal destiny was concerned, my turmoil ceased. I had a sudden inner peace which was to continue with me and sustain me while I was in hospital. This may be inexplicable to the reader, but it was my experience and very real. The conflict was replaced with, 'Songs in the Night'. I looked at the clock, it was 4.00 a.m. I turned over and eventually fell asleep.

Morning beckoned early and realisation of the day's events, already programmed in my mind, surfaced more quickly than the press of a recall button. I lay quietly for a few moments allowing the facts to wash over me, and then I arose and packed a few necessary items for my stay in hospital. This was the last day on earth I would be a physically whole person, but I did believe a day would dawn when my body would arise a spiritual one, perfect in every detail, with no organ missing to make it incomplete.

As the morning wore on, a few friends called, each more sombre than the other. Their feelings of inadequacy to meet the situation evident in their countenance. Sadness and compassion affect our expression, but they enhance our fellow-feeling. These friends, by their very presence, were of enormous help, especially to my mother who was so concerned to see her practical daughter suddenly overwhelmed by the enormity of the situation. Leaving home and leaving my mother so alone and so concerned, broke me when the confirmation of my cancer didn't. I left home in floods of tears, the first and the last I was to shed in this connection.

In hospital, between visitors and ward routine I reflected on what was happening in my life. My thoughts were many and varied, but never sad nor unhappy. In fact I was quite euphoric as I thought over the Lord's plan for my life. The path I was now treading was mapped out by Him before the world was. I saw Him as the Master Planner who knew what He was doing, knew I needed His pruning knife and in this He was treating me as His child. This event in my life was only important insofar as it brought me into contact with Himself and taught me more fully the perfect way.

The realisation that cancer or any other disease could never, of itself, bring about my death was of enormous importance. I saw how I was journeying on to His appointed day and how I would continue to do so, irrespective of disease or of its absence. I saw disease under Divine ordination, not even one cell going askew without His command. Disease of itself cannot terminate life; it does not process death, but it may be, and often is, the vehicle by which God transports the soul into Eternity. Life is terminated by God himself at His appointed time, through means or without means, according to His plan. Why then, I asked myself, did I, and society, view cancer as life threatening? My thoughts were in this channel for many days until His plan came to mean more to me than life itself. It gave, and it continues to give me enormous encouragement and enables me to place cancer in prospective.

It may seem strange to some, but I believed this first episode of cancer to be a punishment for sin. From the outset I had this feeling, and it was confirmed to me the first day I was admitted to hospital. God's word spoke to me with power. 'Wherefore doth a living man complain, a man for the punishment of his sins'. This continued to repeat itself to me until I returned home. What more confirmation could I seek? It was His chastening rod. I have since read that suffering can never be disassociated from sin. We must believe this, for disease and death are the direct result of the Fall. Did this diminish the positive feeling I had about my cancer? In no way. 'It is better to fall into the hands of the living God, than into the hands of man'. I think it is wonderful that He cared enough to speak to me and to deal with me as seemed Him good. 'Shall we take good at the hand of God and not receive evil?'.

Post-operatively, the Lord never left me and my soul rejoiced in His salvation. My first conscious thoughts were these, 'It is of the Lord's mercies that we are not consumed because His compassions fail not. They are new every morning, great is His faithfulness. The Lord is my portion, saith my soul, therefore, will I hope in Him'. Words from the Song of Solomon also addressed themselves to my mind. I never understood their meaning in their application to me at this time. They were in my mind as the consultant walked into my room and because he was a Christian I spoke them aloud. They caused a faint smile to pass over his face, but he offered no comment. The words were these: "We have a little sister and she hath no breasts, what shall we do for our sister in the day when she shall be spoken for?". I spent the evening reading through the Song but the text remained an enigma. I never heard anyone speak on it, but on that day, I simplistically thought I might have to have a second mastectomy.

During the eight days I was in hospital the Lord was indeed my Shepherd. I never wanted for anything. I had inner peace and a great sense of contentment. I thoroughly enjoyed my numerous visitors, even if I did most of the talking. Again, it is difficult for visitors to know what to say when they visit persons with cancer. They feel so sorry for them and so thankful it is not themselves. I was very open with them and shared my experiences, but my happiness unnerved some. It would be easier for them to cope if I were in tears. This would give them something positive to say or do

Others called and told me of this and that person who had survived a number of years after mastectomy. They couldn't understand my indifference to this. I would point out that what was really important to me was His will for my life, whether this meant living or dying. When I said cancer would not bring the day of my death one second closer, they were taken aback. I would then have to explain how we were all travelling on to our appointed time, in health or in sickness. Their reaction fascinated me, for in their eyes, I seemed to be moving towards death while they themselves remained static. I must say these visitors were in the minority.

Back home, I carried on much as I had before. I didn't want my mother worrying about me and so I said little except to give her the result of my pathology. There was no further evidence of carcinogenic cells within the breast tissue or within the lymph glands removed. This delighted her and I overheard her telling one of her friends that I had received the 'all clear'. I had to correct her gently on this in case she might live to see me with 'secondaries'.

I was off work for some time and I wrote everyone who sent cards or flowers and used the opportunity to tell them of the Lord's goodness. This was no mean feat. I had received eighty four cards and twenty eight bouquets of flowers. I knew one of the reasons why I had received so many was the fact that I had cancer. I also knew that people would be more attentive towards what I wrote or said because of this. I, therefore, sought that the Lord would give me an appropriate message for the many who wished me well and were not Christians.

My work brought me into contact with a great many people from many walks of life. This was my opportunity to tell them what God had done for me. No experience is unproductive. In giving me cancer, the Lord knew this and so I wrote officers in the Scottish Office, my peer group and the nuns who served in one of our hospitals, in addition to friends and local colleagues. One colleague wrote telling me how she had once given her heart to the Lord and how she had subsequently backslidden. She said my letter quickened her soul. Eternity alone will tell. The other group who responded were the nuns. The Sister who was the nursing officer, called to see me in my home. She told me how she read the letter out to all the Sisters (religious) and how they were in tears! The outcome of this was that on subsequent visits to their hospital I was invited to say grace and we were able to have a free discussion on biblical issues.

I used at this time to walk each day as far as the big hill in the middle of the croft. There I would sit on a large flat stone and think my thoughts out with my Lord. Diagonally across the inlet of the sea which bordered the croft stood a small family hotel with a public bar. I was very exercised about all our young people who entered its doors. I felt a compulsion to pray for them, and for the unconcerned in our village, as I never had before.

On these lovely June days as my eyes feasted on creation, I used to think I had never seen the hills, the lochs, or the plains quite so beautiful. The scenic view had not changed, but I had. The petty interests that had previously engrossed me had dwindled. It was a wonderful time. The Lord took me apart and He said to me, 'Come and dine', and what a nourishing spiritual diet he set before me! It was a meal of suffering, the spiritual exceeding the physical, overflowing with the love of the Beloved who planned all in covenant love for my soul. Yes, there was music at the feast. There were His 'Songs in the Night' and His word, 'I am their music'. Into my soul broke a certainty that has never been shaken.

Would I rather be without my cancer? Would I prefer never to have had it? A thousand times, No. What! prefer to be without the condition He gifted in His plan for my life over in Eternity? Impossible. It is a privilege. Through it, I drew nigh to Him and He drew nigh to me. I drew nigh because He made it possible for me to do so.

'Draw nigh to God and He will draw nigh to you'.

'My presence shall go with Thee and I will give thee rest'.

chapter eleven

Until The Day Break

'Let me not beg for the stilling of my pains but for the heart to conquer it'.

'Life is always more beautiful than any description', writes J.H. Evans. That being so, my pen cannot possibly capture the Christian character and beauty of the two women whose lives feature in this chapter. Neither can it adequately portray their season of trial, their subsequent descent into the Valley and their joyful expectation of that everlasting city prepared for them in Christ Jesus their Lord. My representation will fall far short of the reality.

The greater reference will be to my mother but I am sure the reader will forgive me. I dwelt in closer proximity to her as we lived out our lives together. Both women, however, touched my life and the lives of many others. The short intricate thread of time had so interwoven our lives that I cannot develop my own account without touching upon theirs.

When I returned to work following the episode of cancer referred to in the previous chapter, my joy was full. As I became involved in my occupation I found myself sucked into all the ups and downs of normal living. Soon I could say with a believer of old, 'when the many occupations of returning health crowd about me, I long for the quiet life

I led with Thee in sickness'. Yet, the experience which so enriched my life I was never to forget. Amidst the many discouragements, the increase of my foes as I fought for principles which were precious to me, and the stubbornness of my own heart, I often returned to the place where God met with me in a special way. But on the occasions when, for example, I fought to maintain tradition relative to Thursday fast day because some of my colleagues, unsympathetic towards these issues, wished to bring about change, it was to the promises He gave me at the outset of my job I went for encouragement. Reflecting on these promises and reminding Him of them often kept me from sinking beneath the load. The Christian cannot be at peace with the enemies of the cause. But the Lord gives deliverance.

Morag kept well for about two years. On papering a room one day she felt a tingling sensation in the middle finger of one hand and shortly afterwards her arm began to swell. A visit to the clinic confirmed the recurrence of her disease. The dark clouds began to gather, but Morag bravely tried to conceal the anxieties which filled her heart. Her children were central in her thoughts, but she was never known to show other than a tranquil spirit. In earnest supplication her heart went forth in prayer to her Lord for her husband and children.

As her illness progressed so the periods of hospitalisation increased. On one such occasion when I called to see her she was in the day room. As I opened the door I saw her surrounded by her family. Her husband was sitting opposite her and her second daughter was sitting on her knee. My heart overflowed in sympathy, temporarily overwhelming me, as I thought on the separation which was to occur, sooner rather than later, within this close-knit family. How difficult it is to relieve anguish and emotional suffering, particularly when children are around. Even when they are not, it is impossible for another person, however close, to experience or understand the vacuum in the lives of those overcome by the sorrow of ancitipated separation. In such circumstances we can but commit loved ones to the consolation of the Holy Spirit in His office as Comforter.

During this time many friends called on the family and Morag's hearty laugh rang forth as she took part in the happy fellowship in her home. The source of her courage was known, yet it was a wonder to many as the months went by. I often identified with her and I wondered, if under the circumstances, I could display the same fortitude. As to her children, she and her husband had received a promise from the Lord that they would be His in the day when He made up His jewels. This was a great comfort to her as she sought to nurture them for the Lord. She prayed for them to the end and she sought God to answer those prayers in His own time.

At this juncture my mother began to complain of a severe and debilitating pain in her right knee. Attributed to rheumatism, within two weeks she had a pathological fracture of the lower end of her femur. The pain was acute. No primary cause could be established. The site of the fracture was awkward and osteoporosis prevented pinning of the bone. A long and painful road lay ahead as efforts were made to promote unification of the fracture.

After my mother had endured traction for three months without evidence of healing, I suggested amputation - having first discussed it with her. This met with astonishment. Amputation on the basis of a fracture is not normal practice, but I had this deep-seated premonition that her femur would never heal and I longed to see her discomfort and immobility relieved. Before her leg broke she had voiced that her condition was but the beginning of the end, which it was, although the journey through the Valley was to take a further four years.

Another five months elapsed before the decision was taken to obtain a biopsy from the fracture site. The findings disclosed a primary sarcoma of bone, not too common a tumour in the elderly. My opinion was sought as to what my mother should be told. "The truth", I said, knowing that nothing less would satisfy her. She was at peace with God's will and would accept the result philosophically. Present when the surgeon told my mother that she had a growth on the bone and the only treatment was amputation, she responded in six words. "My times are in His Hand". After the surgeon left her room I tried to elaborate a little on the procedure, at the same time assuring her that following her operation she would have some degree of mobility. She showed no obvious concern, just a placid acceptance. If her inner thoughts troubled her she did not disclose them. She often said, as she grew older, that she had a lot to suffer before she left this earth. Even after she returned home from hospital I heard her say, "I have a lot to suffer yet before I reach Glory". Perhaps this awareness prepared her to accept each step of her illness. She certainly demonstrated a spirit of reconciliation to what was occurring in her life.

Being in harmony with His will did not mean that she acted super-humanly. No, she had all the frailties of human nature and when provoked responded accordingly. Perfect humanity belongs only to Eternity. What makes God's dealings with His people so precious and the sharing so worthwhile is the manifestation of their faith, their hope and their love in adverse situations. This was certainly in evidence in my mother's life as she descended into the Valley. She was no stranger to enemy attack. Satan frequently buffetted her, but her bouyant hope and the prospect of being forever with her Lord amply sustained her to the end. It could be said that her suffering promoted and deepened her faith in her risen Lord.

A dear friend of her own age wrote her in hospital and I came across the letter recently. It read, "Hello, again! How are you? You don't need pennies for sweets, after all the blessings He has poured on you these last few weeks. No pains left. I hope you are feeling better and that you will soon be home. What wonderful communions they had over there, I hope the Spirit spreads. It would be good to have been amongst the Lord's people. Have you had many visitors recently? It is good that we have Him to go to and that His Promise is that He will never leave us nor forsake us. All blessings." This was written after my mother had her amputation. She and this lady, both of them approaching their eighties, were close friends and a 'peep' at their correspondence left me with a sense of wonderment.

Thirteen months after admission to hospital my mother was discharged home in a wheelchair. An exciting homecoming, yes, but an anxious one too. In the first week or two she felt very vulnerable. Used to so many nurses assisting her, she was concerned that on our own we couldn't cope. She was very sensible about my future, expressing anxiety when I suggested leaving my job to care for her. She was afraid I might not easily find employment suited to my own debility after she was released from the scene of time. The Lord opened the way and we were able to engage two very caring people. Even when one required to leave to care for her own parents, God quickly opened another door. Thus we were able to develop a rota and I was able to continue work. We were to see the Lord's hand in every circumstance of our providence.

While my mother was hospitalised, Morag was a patient on at least three occasions. A nurse used to take her in a wheelchair to visit my mother and what a refreshing time they enjoyed together. They shared aspects of their respective illnesses, cares and concerns, the joy of their salvation and their ultimate expectation. Morag would say, in homely language, "Which of us do you think will be Home first?". On another occasion I heard her say in our mother tongue, "You must not go before me!". My mother would say, "Oh! Morag, you will be in Glory before me, I have a lot to suffer before I enter in". The last time Morag was in hospital she was to say to me, "I will be there before your mother". Their humorous banter, always sprinkled with laughter - Morag had a very easy laugh - left those, like myself, on the periphery, amazed at the naturalness with which the subject of death and Glory was discussed. To the end they knew the drawing power of love to their Lord, and to each other as members of His family. In the words of John Fawcett, they could affirm:

'Blest be the tie that binds
Our hearts in Christian love,
The fellowship of kindred minds
Is like to that above'.

Visiting Morag in her ward she used to say, "It would be a blessing if your mother was taken Home, away from all her sufferings". In her own terminal state, Morag was still able to think of others. A truly Christian spirit!

Without fail on a Monday she would ask me, "Were the children in Church yesterday?". Her next question was "What were the girls wearing?". On one such occasion I said they were wearing anoraks. She seemed unhappy about this, and said, "Their aunt gave them these as a present, they weren't meant to wear them to church". Even on the brink of Glory she was anxious that her children would continue in the practices in which they were taught.

On her last visit to hospital she was rather unwell and as I approached her bedside she said in Gaelic,

'But yet at length out of them all
The Lord shall set him free'.

The reference was to the ultimate deliverance from affliction which the Lord had appointed for His children. I took up her theme, knowing she knew, as I did, that her sojourn among us was almost over.

Expressing a desire to die at home, one of her sisters promised to care for her, which she did. This was a blessed time for her and it meant enormous support to the husband and the children, who at eleven, thirteen and fourteen, were still of tender years. What feelings of protectiveness I experienced towards these children, who were so composed throughout the whole event. They were kept by the power of prayer.

An interesting phenomenon was reported by those attending Morag's funeral procession. As they slowly winded their way along the village road, they were aware of singing wafting, as it were, towards them. We in the homestead heard nothing. It was only when the men returned from the cemetery that we heard of this incident. They were of the opinion that those in the home must have been singing. It was only when they realised that this was not so that the significance of what they heard came home to them. What singing must have greeted Morag when she entered her heavenly abode when such angelic singing accompanied her mortal remains.

In the week in which the Rev. J.A. James lost his wife he took up his Bible to conduct family worship and said, "Notwithstanding the events of this week, I see no reason to depart from our usual practice of reading in Psalm 103". He proceeded, "Bless the Lord, O my soul, and all that is within me bless His holy name". This was grace in action and it was the spirit Morag's husband manifested at the time of her departure and in the days which lay ahead.

When I informed my mother of Morag's death she said quite simply, "Nach math dhith", (Isn't she fortunate), and she meant it. She really missed her, particularly so on her return from hospital. The frequent 'phone calls to each other, so much part of her life before she went into hospital, were forever over. In the few years my mother lived after Morag we often talked of her and we enjoyed many visits from her godly husband. Their daughters, with two of their friends, were, in time, to form a rota whereby they came and sat with my mother each Sabbath evening, so that I could attend church. This was a sweet gesture on their part and my heart knit in love to these youngsters and I have never lost my affection for them. Three of them are now members of the church and I am confident that the fourth, in His time, will also be converted.

For almost three years the routine established in our home provided a sense of normal daily living. There were the seasons of discouragement, but there were also the mountain top experiences. My mother's meat and drink was the word of God. From the time I first took note of her spiritual activity her practice was consistent. In this she differed hugely from myself. Not given to doubts, she dismissed them as dishonouring to God and never wasted time discussing them with friends who might be thus afflicted. For many years prior to her death she was unable to attend church. When I could not relay the service because my mind had wandered at this or that point, she would openly rebuke me. When she went to church, she would say, she went to listen and she gave the service her full attention, and I believe she did. A disciplined Christian herself, she had little time or sympathy for those of us who were out of line.

The application of truth to her mind was interesting and to her as manna. A verse of scripture would surface in her thoughts. She would look it up in the Word, examine the context and then find out what Matthew Henry had to say about it. She would explore what was in her mind when the verse presented itself or what she had been praying for or about. She always prayed about the verse and then she waited for the Lord either to fulfill His promise or to give her another truth by which she could verify what she understood Him to be saying. Through this process the Lord often revealed His will to her. He never failed her and I never knew a prediction, based on what He revealed to her, to be wrong. I used to say to her, "If a verse of Truth is in my mind, I think it is there only because it is known to me". "The Truth", she would say, "never presents itself without a purpose. Nurture it".

She certainly did. I remember her being quite distressed because the Lord had not spoken to her through His Truth for a week or two. She would rather He spoke in rebuke than not at all.

As she grew older, fearful that she might forget, she wrote down the spoken truth immediately on whatever piece of paper was to hand at the time. I found texts written on just about everything, from scrap paper to matchboxes and even on the packaging of a pair of butt hinges. I am sorry I never retained these, although I do have one or two, found in the pages of her favourite Spurgeon's sermons. In the handwriting of our two helpers, these must have been written towards the end of her life. The butt hinges, still in their packaging, carry the following verse, in Gaelic.

'For thou art gracious, O Lord,
And ready to forgive
And rich in mercy, all that call
Upon thee to relieve'.

It must have been written before she took ill. I found the hinges on the top shelf of a cupboard which it would be quite impossible for her to reach from her wheelchair. More recently, in the pages of an old book, I found a slip of paper on which she had written in Gaelic, not a text, but these words, literally translated, 'Lord, is it not Thyself that is worthy of being believed at all times' and then in English, 'Jesus loves me'.

In the springtime of the year she died she said to me one evening as we sat by the fire together, "I was thinking this afternoon how lonely you would be in the winter time, coming home from work to a cold, empty house with no meal prepared". At the time, though infirm, her health gave no reason for increased concern. Her remark threw me. I knew she knew she would not see another winter. She was trying to prepare me for what was soon to be a reality. Age does not diminish a mother's feelings towards her family, even when mature in years. In her reflections she had entered into the loneliness she knew I would experience and she felt deeply for me. Even saints on the brink of Glory find parting from loved ones painful. As with other discussions which touched me personally, I lost the preciousness of the moment by my response. I did not wish her to see how deeply I was affected.

As she entered into the terminal phase of her illness, she experienced a great sense of loneliness. This is not uncommon. I used to be very interested in gardening and as spring gave way to early summer I would spend an hour or two each evening weeding or watering plants in the greenhouse. She would say when I came home from work, "Don't go out tonight, stay in with me, I feel so lonely". Could I have discerned it, I would have known she was but brief weeks from Eternity, but at the time she seemed reasonably well.

Death was always an open subject with us and as her health began slowly to deteriorate we often talked about it, even in the presence of her general practitioner. At this time the senior partner in the practice was himself unwell. He was the doctor present when I was told of my cancer and had been our general practitioner for many years. My mother always asked after his health when her doctor called. Both he and my mother died within two weeks of each other. Our dialogue about death, dying and the hereafter was to us very natural and it made a great impression on our general practitioner. I heard her afterwards remark that she had used our experience in an address she had given on the mainland. It brought home to me the importance of being positive Christians in the face of adversity, particularly when unconverted persons are present. We little know what God may use or bless and our lives speak volumes on our death bed, especially if we retain our faculties. Someone once said that dying was the last thing we could do for our Lord and we should do it well. 'Sickness', Spurgeon writes, 'yields large tribute to the King's revenue, if it be we may cheerfully endure it'.

One thing was very evident in her life, particularly so in the last months, maybe even in the last year. She had a constant desire after holiness. In her prayers at worship she could be heard earnestly seeking sanctification and in her discussions she often referred to her great need to be sanctified. She accepted her sufferings as part of the process of sanctification and readily agreed that the Lord could sanctify the soul in the twinkling of an eye. Nevertheless, she was concerned that her shortcomings and the sinfulness of her heart would hinder this work. Another interesting observation was the way in which she ended her prayers. "Lord", she would say in Gaelic, "give us a place in Thine intercession".

Notified that two of her nieces from Brazil were to visit us shortly, I decided to renovate our small sitting room. One evening after I had helped my mother to bed, she said to me, "What have you done with the carpet you lifted off the floor of the small sitting room?". To my answer she responded "Don't dispose of it until the room is complete in case anything happens to me". Assuring her that if this did happen I wouldn't necessarily require the small room, she bluntly said, "I would like the house in order at the time of my wake". Concerned that this was a premonition I called next morning on the contractor, the painter and the man in the carpet shop and informed them of the situation. Within one week the work was complete. A tremendous display of goodwill.

Two days after my mother spoke with such conviction I was transferring her from her Parker Knoll chair into her wheelchair when she calmly said, "Did you hear that crack?" "Yes", I said. "Well", she went on, "that was my arm". Sure enough, she had a pathological fracture of her forearm. From then on she could not be physically managed by one person. With a lesion manifesting itself in her lung causing her acute breathing difficulties, her sufferings increased, yet I never heard her complain, but I did hear her say to friends who called to see her, "This" - referring to her sufferings - "is the road to Glory". On another occasion she was asked by two elderly Christians if she longed for the Lord to take her with Himself. "No", she responded, "I am content to await His time, but when He comes I will be happy to go".

She was delighted to get back into the small sitting room, for which she had chosen both carpet and wall covering. She absolutely amazed me with her avid interest in everything around her, despite being so unwell. The evening the workmen finished she said to me, "I am so pleased you got that done". "Yes", I said, "so am I, for I couldn't face doing it after you are gone". "The Brazilians", she went on, "will come, but I will not see them". "I had hoped you might be with me for some time yet", I said. "You might get your wish", she replied, "but I don't think so". Another evening I heard her say, "I don't think it will be long now, events I sought from God are beginning to happen". She never expanded further, but I thought I understood to what she referred. It was at this time, one morning as I brought in her breakfast, she said, "I saw the late Mr. MacIver of Carloway in my sleep last night and he called me twice by name". This minister had been many years in Glory at the time. In fact I had no recollection of ever seeing him. I was to remember this dream after she herself had been transported to Glory.

One afternoon as her birthday drew near, I was putting the final touches to her cake, when two friends called to see her. As they observed what I was doing I said to them, "I'm not sure that she will live to see her birthday", to which John replied in his genial way, "If not, we will call it her Glory cake!" Concerned as to what I was doing, the air of secrecy suddenly reminded her and when I entered her bedroom she said, "Were you decorating the cake?" - The ward staff celebrated her birthday when she was in hospital and I baked a cake for the occasion. This continued to be my practice after she returned home. - "Yes", I said. "Do you think I will see it?", meaning her birthday, she then asked. In honesty I replied, "I'm not sure, judging by your condition at present it doesn't seem too likely". She was quiet for a few minutes, and a thought occurred to me. "Would you like to see it", I said. A great baker in her day, she said "Yes". As she admired it I said "I'm glad you saw it just in case we do not have the opportunity to see it together again". But we did. For about two hours she was well enough to take an interest in her flowers and cards and along with the district nurse, our helper, and myself, to enjoy a cup of tea and a small slice of cake. She made a great effort to be what she probably felt very unlike. She said to me, "I'm glad for your sake I was well enough to join in". It was Friday morning. The following Wednesday Glory broke upon her gaze. In the words of Blaise Pascal, who is said to have suffered intensely on his death bed, my mother's prayers can be summed up, "Sick as I am, may I glorify You in my suffering".

Two days before she died I was in alone when she asked to be positioned more comfortably. Finding it difficult to do so on my own I prayed, as I had done on previous occasions, that the Lord would send someone to help me so that I wouldn't have to trouble the district nurse or our helper who had just left. Two people called who very willingly assisted me. Offering her a drink, one of these good friends sat her up while I fed her. Touching her face in the process and remarking, "Your face is very cold", she haltingly replied, "I will soon be cold all over".

Somewhat overcome, I said, "What will we do without you". "Oh!", she said, "you have a Throne of Grace to go to, take all your troubles there and place the house in His care whenever you leave it". She then diverted my attention by requesting some Benger's food. I felt she dismissed me for a reason and she did. While I was in the kitchen she said to her two visitors, "When I am gone, don't forget Chrissie, remember to call on her". When I was told of this I concluded that she had spoken for the last time. She had. It wouldn't really have mattered whom the Lord sent that evening, she would have discharged her burden for me on to them. It was her last motherly act before she slept in Jesus.

Our minister and his predecessor's widow called just as my mother took her leave of this earth. They were on their way to the weekly prayer meeting. It was then I heard for the first time a story which linked in with my mother's recent dream. Apparently she was assisting in the manse on the occasion when she first sat at the Lord's table. On the morning of the Lord's Day the minister's wife on going upstairs found my mother weeping in her room. Enquiring as to the reason for her distress, my mother simply said, "I have denied my Lord". Advising the minister of my mother's troubled state he, on confirming the reason, conferred with the two visiting ministers. They agreed that the session should be constituted and indicated their willingness to participate. This was unusual but the advanced hour necessitated such measures. My mother thus met with the session and was received into full membership of the church. The desire of her heart to sit, that morning, at the Lord's Table in response to His command, 'This do in remembrance of me', was fulfilled. The presiding minister at the morning service, and one of those present at the session, was the minister who called her by her name in the dream she saw the week before she died. She had never shared this unique experience with me and as I heard of it I had an overwhelming desire to go into her bedroom and ask her about it, but she was gone, forever gone from the scene of time.

chapter twelve

Alone

'Hindered a while, and in a wilderness I walked alone.'

When my parents were married they received an unusual telegram from an elderly couple who were friends of my father. It is found in Ruth 4:11 & 12. "The Lord make the woman that is come into thine house like Rachael and like Leah which two did build the house of Israel .... And let thy house be like the house of Pharez ... of the seed which the Lord shall give thee of this young woman". I used to tease my mother, as the years passed and I never married, that the sentiments of this telegram could never be fulfilled. She always had a ready answer.

Despite her light-hearted approach, my solitary situation troubled my mother a great deal as she closed in with death. This was evident, not only to myself, but to those close to her. The family friend who wrote a tribute to her in the local paper commented thus '.... For those of us privileged to witness our friend's latter days, to listen to her words of wisdom, her resignation as she approached the end and her sound advice to her only daughter for whom she expressed concern in a most touching way, we can honestly say it was good for us to have been there. Israel, as he was about to die, encouraged his son Joseph with the words, 'Behold I die, but God shall be with you'. With this same assurance my mother sought to console me as the light of her life dimmed and went out. What greater legacy could she have left me? I did believe He would be with me and that He would answer my mother's prayers and seven years later I can testify to this, but at the time the pain of loneliness and separation was intensified by the greater pain of a journey through the remainder of my life humanly alone. Previous bereavement had shown me that things are never the same after the death of a loved one; but this was quite different. In it I knew the unparalleled emotions associated with the parting of a sole close relative. Without family there was no division of grief or of isolation. Those entirely alone have a unique providence, not often understood by friends or society, or even by those who live alone but are part of an extended family group.

Immediately after my mother's funeral and in the days that followed, I was acutely sensitive to the fact that there was no one with whom I could share my grief, no one who could break the stifling silence of my home, no one who could fathom the depth of my solitude or who could channel my thoughts in a different direction. Consequently, the acute phase of the grief process extended beyond that which is considered the norm. My constant prayer became, "Lord, let me sin not in my grief". It is very hard to explain these feelings to someone who has never experienced them.

Another facet of being alone, is how much more difficult it is to shake off pressing thoughts. When I used to come home from work burdened by some problem, I either shared it, if I could, or else I forced myself to be sociable. Either way the problem was halved. Now these same problems absorb my thinking all evening or even into the night. Family have a place in our lives we do not even pause to consider. They assist in our well-being. Our cares become their cares and are embraced by them to our betterment. Friends are wonderful, but we keep back the part of ourselves we share with family. We cannot have the absolute freedom or the unique closeness enjoyed within the family unit. Scripture teaches us, 'Trust ye not in a friend'. Perplexing words, but they are probably in Holy Writ to draw our attention to the fact that friends may be close to us today and off the horizon of our lives tomorrow. Imperfect as the family relationship may be, God intended this to be the ideal framework within which we humans could extend ourselves and know liberty, free from constraint. Friends cannot remain indefinitely in our company. They must return to the nucleus of their own families, drawn there by an irresistible power. From this we can rightly deduce that for those bereft of family there will always be a missing link, however adjusted and however reconciled, by God's Grace, we become to our circumstances.

In these early days, aloneness created a sense of loss and sorrow which left me yearning for companionship. It was quite different from the thirteen years I had lived alone earlier in my life. I appreciated this as freedom, but then I had only to pick up the telephone to be linked with home. Now there were moments when it seemed, as someone else put it, 'as if I had been left with no one on earth to love me'. I would then talk to my Lord aloud and in my heart, I still do, and tell Him exactly how I felt. I would tell Him I needed Him in a special way, that I now had no one of my own and no one who would bear me in prayer to a Throne of Grace as my mother had, I would tell Him I needed His love, needed His companionship and needed to know and feel His nearness. Oh! the fervency with which I talked with Him when aloneness became an overwhelming burden.

I recently read of one in similar circumstances who wrote, ".... on being given loved ones who showed tenderness to me, I was to say, "O my God, in the midst of my happiness I often forget Thee. My thoughts converse with my human loved ones and less and less with Thee .... I deserve that Thou should'st make me lonely again". Later the same anonymous author wrote, ".... is it not Thee Lord who alone knowest how little I deserve to be loved and yet Thou lovest me better than all; surrounded by a thousand friends life would be solitude but for Thee". The author is honest in his description of the effect loved ones had upon him, nonetheless, this should not undermine the value we place on family and friends in our daily living. We sin in every circumstance. Family can wean us from Him, aloneness or singleness can wean us from Him. Conversely, these circumstances can draw us to Him. There is no state on earth in which we can give ourselves perfectly to Him. But we must remember it was the God who fashioned us in His own image, who created us and who at all times knows us better than we know ourselves, who said, 'It is not good for man to be alone'. This is why being without family can in fact be a cross. It was not God's order in the beginning and human hearts reach out to be fulfilled in the manner of companionship God has ordained. There is nothing wrong with this. But in the comprehension of what God has ordered for my own life, I see no confusion. It is His favoured plan, covenanted in Eternity before the generations of my people were ever thought off. Surely it is therefore good, even when, in human fashion, I alternate between commitment to His Will and a longing for companionship which drives me straight into His bosom.

During the early days of my solitude I had an unusual conflict, prompted, I am sure, by Satan. Why, he whispered, was I the last of the line on a croft occupied for generations by my people? Why had I never married and had children of my own to surround me or to carry on the line of the family? Why did all my uncles emigrate to South America, never to return, adopting a foreign land as their homeland with none of them or their families, as far as can be ascertained, showing evidence of faith? I floundered for some time over these issues. This may sound strange, but perhaps it will be better understood when it is realised that my real temptation was in relation to the Commandment '.... I the Lord thy God am a jealous God, visiting the iniquity of the fathers upon the children unto the third and fourth generation ....'. Was this what happened in my family? Did iniquity, in a past generation, provoke God to righteous anger? I thought of Old Testament families where punishment was meted out to the extinction of stock. For myself there could never, in time, be an answer to these questions. I turned them all over to Him and in doing so I saw the Eternal Covenant, the mere good pleasure of God's Will and with this I was and am content.

On the day of my mother's funeral I received a postcard from London announcing the arrival of my Brazilian cousins in two weeks time. Much as I felt the need to belong to someone, this anticipated visit filled me with concern. I had never met them, but I knew we were of a different religion and a different language. In a telephone call, prior to their arrival, I informed them of my mother's death. They were acutely disappointed, especially so, as their visit could have been earlier. Their mother was of Spanish/Argentinian stock and they decided to visit Spain before coming to Lewis.

As the day of their arrival approached, my early concerns surfaced. I was aware that one cousin had been treated for a malignant melanoma, but a hurried letter before their arrival warned me not to speak of disease, as this was their way of dealing with it. Because I did not know them I resolved to go along with this, which meant I could not freely talk of my mother. I decided to shut out her death entirely until after their visit. For me it was a hyper-sensitive area and I could not open up with strangers of perhaps a different temperament and of divergent views. Though I knew we were cousins I thought of them as acquaintances never met. I wondered how we would interact. Would we recognise kinship instantly, would a family feeling exist, would we like each other and 'gel' together? A host of thoughts flooded my mind. How, would I introduce grace before meals, family worship and the services of the Lord's Day. I fervently wished my mother was alive. Such matters would present no difficulty to her. Suddenly I felt vulnerable and alone.

This disquietude awoke a further train of thought. My mother had always led the conversation when Christian friends called, and during spiritual gatherings in our home, her opinion was often sought. I had a tendency to sit and listen, aware that my mother was a spiritually exercised woman. I felt such a novice and at this point quite inadequate. Suddenly, I became concerned that the Lord's people would cease to visit the home, that it would not be the Bethel to them it once was. I began to pray that my understanding would be opened, that I would be given the power of utterance, that the Lord would delight to visit His Sion, in what was now my home. In reality, I was praying that I would receive a double portion of my mother's spirit, as Elisha had sought from Elijah when he was about to die. I wanted, rightly or wrongly, her mantle to fall on me, not, I freely confess, for my own glory but to carry forward His work. I did not pause to think that there might be a cross in the way. Our petitions can be so glib. We ask for what we understand not and that without considering the way in which the Lord may answer us. Are we ready to bear whatever He may require of us in the receipt of deeper commitment and spirituality? We must be disciplined Christians; there is a big army against us, the world, the flesh and the devil.

In the throes of these thoughts my anxieties about the Brazilians' visit fled. I had arranged to meet them in Inverness and to travel back to Lewis with them. Ascending the stair of the hotel, I was aware of the lift doors closing on the ground floor, and then I heard my name being called. I turned round and there they were. I was amazed that they recognised me, particularly as they could only view me from behind. They were with me for only three days, but we crammed a lot into them. Grace was easy, worship was easy and the question of the Lord's Day was resolved by their request to attend services in the church of their father's youth. Had I not taken a stand on these issues from the first meal and the first night, it might not have been so easy to undertake it later.

The cousin who had had the melanoma used to stay up after her sister retired to bed. During this time she questioned me as to my mother's illness and as to my own. How was I to respond, having been warned not to engage in such a conversation? I did so by being direct. As a consequence she spoke openly of her own ill-health and there were absolutely no barriers in our frankness with one another. I felt my heart go out to her with particular warmth. Here was a woman who had cancer, but no saving faith whereby she could take courage from a relationship with the Lord. How could I speak with her without giving offence? Realising that one of her Christian names was that of our aunt who had died when I finished my training, I addressed her thus, "You have been named after a godly woman who is now in Glory. How wonderful if, like her, you came to know the Saviour and to spend Eternity in the same Everlasting City". Continuing in this vein I told her a little about Chirsty and my mother and how they faced death with expectation. I was then able to exhort her gently. She never said a word but listened intently and I knew she was affected. The atmosphere was encouraging. As she arose to go to bed she embraced me and later returned to the room and, taking off her necklace gave me the heart shaped pendant, saying, "This is to show you we have taken you to our hearts". I was really touched and longed deeply - and still do - that she would come to know the Lord. For her there would be many difficulties in the way. I knew this and I am sure she did. Like Agrippa she was an, "almost persuaded" Christian. Today she resides in

Florida, the effects of that evening long forgotten in the stream of daily living. I gave each of them a Bible as we parted, but I do realise that while they read English, doing so is an effort. I do not expect they ever opened it but I keep hoping the day may come when they will.

While with me they encouraged me to visit Brazil. My mother's death had occurred less than three weeks previously and although outwardly calm, the shadow of parting from those who had shared my home for but three short days filled me with forebodings of loneliness. Yes, I would go to Brazil, the need to identify with family was strong. Three months later I embarked on the long journey to South America. I flew from Stornoway to Glasgow and via London and Amsterdam to Rio de Janeiro, and later to São Paulo. It may have seemed long, but it was short in point of time and adventure, by comparison with my uncles who had emigrated and journeyed by ship in the early nineteen twenties. I wondered what my mother would have said if she was alive. I think she would have been reluctant to let me go, the memories of the 'twenties with its inevitable heartache would have pressed sorely upon her. But at this time my overwhelming desire was to be anchored within family and as I prepared to go I gave little thought to the cultural and other differences which might exist between us. I soon realised how unprepared I was. Some cousins spoke little or no English, but even those who could do so reasonably well resorted to Portugese in my presence. The language was a great barrier. It excluded me from the very close knit relationship I perceived to exist. In addition, there was the barrier of religion. My Christian beliefs, my faith, my sensitivity to the Lord's Day, separated me from them. I felt they were disappointed in the first Scottish cousin they had ever met.

There were other differences, our interests, for example, and the cultural variations which ranged from politics to poverty and to riches, to say nothing of the many nationalities who, through marriage, were now family. I sought with difficulty to find one or two who resembled their Island forebears. Despite the blood tie and the prevalence of Scottish names and my maternal surname, I felt we were strangers. There was much I had to learn and too short a time in which to learn it and I came away feeling I did not belong.

Often during this holiday I thought of the uncles whose progeny they were. I could understand why my uncles left the Island, but I could never understand why they chose a country so far removed and so different to their Island roots, to say nothing of the home environment in which they were brought up. I was quite bewildered by the fact that they had remained there, entered into mixed marriages and totally accepted the way of life of their adopted country. Did I and the cousins I met really have the same grandparents? Heredity is an interesting study.

My feelings of isolation were many times accentuated during this visit. I did not leave them behind at home as I expected I would. One reason for this was the fact that I went too soon after my mother's death. While I was there I would suddenly think, I must remember to tell my mother this, or, my mother would be interested in that, only to recall that she was forever removed from the scene of time. I never thought I would ever return to that country, but I did. Three years later I was back. I wanted to be a 'missionary' to my own people and on the first morning I awoke there it was the Lord's Day. My eyes opened to a beautiful morning. We were staying for the weekend at the farm in Mendes miles away from Rio with its bustling traffic. The cockerel was crowing and there was a peace and quietude, when the words, 'How shall I sing the Lord's song in a strange land' fell into my thoughts. I felt deeply burdened as I arose and dressed. I longed for the day to pass so as to avoid sinning our way through a Day which God exhorts us to keep Holy. I prayed for wisdom, for knowledge, for understanding and for opportunity. God afforded me the opportunity I sought, but sadly it bore no fruit. Of this visit I can certainly say I felt more connected, but there remained huge differences between us. It did cement relationships, with some more than others, and I am glad I went.

Following my first visit to Brazil I went to Switzerland and the Holy Land, all within the same year. Well meaning friends used to say, perhaps a little in envy, I now had the freedom to go anywhere I pleased, when I pleased. Indeed I did, but these comments hurt. They revealed how little my friends understood a life lived out alone. My new found liberty I could live without, but I found it difficult to live without family. My spirit was not free. For years I had telephoned every day when I was away from home, both to alleviate my mother's anxiety and to assure myself of her well-being. Now I could go to the ends of the earth; I required to confer with no-one, to be anxious about no-one. By the same token there was no-one anxious about me. It mattered not where I went, what I was doing or if I did nothing. Anxiety, normal to human beings, can be a productive emotional activity, provided it is not excessive and it is channelled aright. When it cannot be experienced within the framework of family, because family does not exist, the result is a terrible void. These holidays were but a reaching out, an effort to fill the vacuum with human interaction.

Well might the reader ask, as I detail these sterile feelings and reactions, where my Lord was in all this. He was, as He promised, Father to the fatherless and Helper to the helpless. He was very dear to me for He was my all. I continued to converse with Him aloud in my home and in the car. I committed the house to Him, seeking that it might be a Bethel to the souls of the Lord's people, not only while I was alive, but after my death. Many would say. Does it matter what happens then? I think it does. We have a responsibility to leave our affairs in order and without relatives it is hard to foresee who may occupy and use the things from which we and the Lord's people received solace and that over many years. I would dearly love my home, while block upon block remains, to be occupied by His people, and I dearly hope that after I am gone my executors will see to this. This is another difficulty for those without close relatives. Every small item becomes a burden as one seeks to leave one's earthly possessions in such a way as to make their disposal easy for those concerned. One is conscious that it is outsiders who will dispense with the contents of one's home and personal belongings and it is a bounden duty to leave things in an orderly fashion. There are also the arrangements post death to be seen to. I have left written instructions regarding this, so that no-one will be in any doubt as to what to do. There are a host of things which touch the lives of those bereft of family that are never even thought of by those who live within a family unit.

Despite the cloud of painful feelings which these and other matters generated, the Lord did not hide Himself, but remained faithful to His promises. 'Behold I die, but God shall be with you' - He was, 'I will never leave Thee nor forsake Thee' - He never has, 'God is our refuge and our strength' - He has been. 'I the Lord thy God will hold thy right hand, saying unto thee, fear not: I will help Thee' - He has held it and helped. All the promises are ours, and faithful is He who promiseth. I would not like anyone reading this chapter to think that God hid His face from me at this time. He was very much with me, even when my reactions and feelings were at their most human. In the first year as I tried to come to terms with my solitary state and I used to yearn for companionship, I would nuzzle closer to Himself. He ultimately gave me my desire for companionship, not as I sought, but as He willed. Within a year of my mother's death my companion was a secondary progression of my cancer, my first bone metastasis.

chapter thirteen

The Furnace For Gold

'Glory to Thee for all the grace I have not tasted yet'.

The coach trip from Zurich airport was a getting-to-know-each-other experience. An assemblage of fifty persons. We had flown in from London and were heading for the Bernese Oberland on a group holiday with a Christian organisation.

The weather was marvellous, the group very friendly and the scenery absolutely awe-inspiring. Lakes, blue and green in colour, vast ranges of snow-capped mountains, glaciers and alpine flowers, all added to the wonders of God's creation in this country. The valleys, shaken by avalanches of rocks and enormous ice blocks, as they thundered down the slopes of mountain ranges thousands and thousands of years before, presented a natural environment breathtaking in its loveliness and a haven for walkers. With some of the group, strangers until a few days previously, I enjoyed many walks, charmed by the beauty of our idyllic surroundings. Without warning my pleasure in this simple activity was soon to be cut short.

Bible study was a big part of this holiday conference and I found myself unusually moved by the theme the preacher took. I at first associated my reaction with my mother's death, but I then perceived that God was dealing with me and I had a heightened awareness of some impending trial. Four days into the holiday I developed a pain in my left hip which I took to be the result of excessive exercise. Walking was now reduced to a minimum, but the pain did not recede and I began to have doubts that the cause was quite as simple as I at first thought.

I made many friends on this trip and as we parted one from another and I returned to the Island, I felt quite homesick. But in addition to friendship I had another legacy - pain and a feeling of foreboding. By the time I sought medical aid I was thoroughly convinced of the origin of the pain. This was made known to me through the truth, the bent of my thoughts and the progressive nature of the pain itself. My mind was stayed on Him and He kept me in perfect peace.

September was approaching its latter days. The communion season had come and gone. The leaves were beginning to fall off the trees and early autumnal changes were in evidence when I made my way to the doctor's surgery. The usual investigative procedures were arranged and undertaken, but neither physical examination nor the series of X-rays revealed any abnormality. The pain increased in severity and I was referred to a Consultant of Phsyical Medicine. It was his opinion that my problem stemmed from an arthritic lumbar vertebra. Physiotherapy was arranged, but I cancelled the arrangements, outlining my difficulty in accepting the diagnosis. Movement was now extremely painful. Still I went ahead with a cordon bleu course for which I had enrolled, but it was with exceeding difficulty I carried on normally. One evening as I left the college, I could hardly walk to my car. Driving was a problem and although it was late I stopped off at the doctor's surgery. There was still no accounting for my pain. God's time was not yet and I must patiently await until He revealed all. The furnace had not been heated to the point of refining.

Spring approached and the crocus' pushed their white, mauve and yellow heads through the awakened soil. I glanced around, as I painfully tried to walk the few steps from the house to the garage. The trees, still in their infancy, could be seen putting forth their buds. The season of hope, of life, of vitality, of production was upon us. I sighed. Would I ever see these trees reach maturity? I thought not. I looked forward with expectation, not to springtime bursting forth with fresh energy, but to the fulfillment of God's plan. When would He intervene? When would the expectation I had of relief from pain, through the treatment of radiotherapy, be effected? By now I fully expected this to be the outcome, especially following the incident when, as I looked out the kitchen window, the force of thought made me utter aloud, "if you received radiotherapy that pain would go away". I firmly believed what was planted in my mind.

March, the month of our spring communions was now upon us. How could I see the weekend through? I was accustomed to many visitors. Could I undertake the necessary preparations? Small things, taken so much for granted, had long since become a problem. At weekends household chores such as lighting the fire were difficult to accomplish. Could I carry in the bucket of coal? Could I get down on my knees or get up again? When a task was achieved I felt so thankful to my Lord. In fact "Lord, help me" and "Lord, thank you", never left my lips. I recall one afternoon, at the communion weekend, going to feed the hens. A short incline led to the hen-house - where were all these inclines before? I had never noticed them. Progress was very slow, very difficult and pain tore at my heart. With tears falling I prayed, "Lord, help me to get there", and on my return, "Lord, help me to reach the house". This may seem incredible, but it is true. Morag, not the Morag already referred to in this book, but the lady who used to be my mother's helper and whom I had kept on after she died, called unexpectedly. Watching me she approached and assisted. I sat on the kitchen chair and wept with the pain. After a short break I reached the sitting room and sat without moving all evening until I went to bed. I could not go to Church and no one visited, for which I felt thankful as I could not easily get about. I called on the Lord and placed my anxieties before Him. "Lord, help me through this weekend", and He did - wondrously.

The Lord's Day was communion day. I did manage to Church. Would I see another communion weekend? These were natural thoughts and their application to my mind practical rather than fearful. It was lovely to be in the Lord's House with His people and equally delightful to have His people in my home for lunch. Among those who came was someone who helped me serve the lunch and wash up. The

Lord is so faithful to His Children, more obvious in time of need. He never lets us down, though we so often fail Him. After lunch and before anyone left the table, one of the more senior men asked for a Bible and requested the singing of Psalm 45, in Gaelic, commencing at verse 13:

> *'Behold the daughter of the King*
> *All glorious is within:*
> *And with embroideries of gold*
> *her garments wrought have been'.*

There were several male singers at the table and so they passed the Psalmody along from one to another and sang the remaining verses. Something seemed to descend upon the company in the singing of:

> *'They shall be brought with gladness great,*
> *And mirth on every side,*
> *Into the palace of the King,*
> *And there they shall abide'.*

Tears streamed from almost every eye present. I thought to myself "This is wonderful, I must be going to die". I never applied the circumstances to anyone present but myself. On returning home that Sabbath evening the wife of the gentleman who asked for the singing of these words, suddenly passed into Eternity. The Lord was preparing him and comforting him in advance of the sore trial which awaited him, yet, none of us had the spiritual perception to recognise this.

Was I frustrated by the delay in my diagnosis? Not at all. I understood the Lord's purpose to be wise and true. His plan is perfect. 'The furnace for gold'. The point of refinement had still not been reached. He had to educate me in many matters and I must wait patiently upon Him. I knew He knew what He was doing and that in His time He would reveal the true nature of my symptoms and the medical profession would be afforded the opportunity of diagnosis. We must see all from His side. He is in everything. This was the way I had to walk, the thorny path of pain, but my Lord was with me, teaching His stubborn child His Will. Strangely, I never felt the time long, but the process certainly kept me reliant upon Himself. Day by day, when help was required, He assisted me. Amidst it all I was thankful my mother was spared the sorrow of seeing me suffer and though it meant I was humanly alone, I never felt alone at this time. 'He filled my life with pain and my conversation with Himself.'

I shared little with friends. Their responses were exactly as pre-dicted. They tried to dissuade me in my thinking. It could not possibly be, not nine years after a mastectomy, as if this excluded further progression of the disease. My increasing lameness had to be an arthritic hip joint. Such disbelief - or was it that they themselves could not face the facts? - was very frustrating. From then on my conclusions remained sealed in my heart. There was little point in sharing. Time, I knew, would soon reveal everything to everyone, myself included.

My senses now told me that matters were coming to a head. One morning, as with difficulty I tried to dress, I had an innate feeling I might soon be in hospital. I could not now sneeze or cough without a seering pain shooting through the affected area. I went back to my general practitioner, telling him I was not seeking a cure, but a diagnosis. He listened to the account of my increasing symptoms and said, "I do not think we can exclude a metastasis. I will arrange for further X-rays. If these are negative, I will refer you to an Orthopaedic Surgeon". It was the first time the word metastasis was mentioned. I must pause here to admit that despite my own assurances over a lengthy period that this was the true nature of my condition, the word still held a kind of ominous ring when the doctor suggested it. It confirmed the road I must now go down. The week following I was in very slow motion. I still went to work and did everything required of me. I had, up to this point, attended meetings in Edinburgh as necessary. My colleagues, gathered for these meetings, attended on the progression of my illness with interest and concern. I well knew their unspoken thoughts - my disease was again active. With hindsight it is amazing, even to myself, that I was able to continue travelling as I did. God was certainly with me in this testing time.

One Friday, realising the extent of my pain, a colleague took action on my behalf. Visiting hospital on a work related matter he met the Locum Surgeon, who was covering annual leave for the regular Consultant, and shared with him my difficulties. He agreed to see me after the plaster clinic, obviating the need to await my outpatient appointment the following Tuesday. Actually it was an intervention for which I felt extremely thankful. After the usual clinical and X-ray examinations I saw the Consultant again. He came straight to the point. The findings were suspicious. "Is it your opinion", I asked, "that what you see on X-ray is a bone secondary?". "That would be my view", he responded, "but come along to the duty room and I will 'phone the Consultant Radiologist". He put on the kettle, 'phoned this mainland Consultant and engaged him in a clinical dialogue. Sitting there I heard precisely his views on my condition. He then prepared coffee for us both, at the same time dictating a letter to my general practitioner. I knew no-one else knew more than I did and this frankness I will ever appreciate.

Over coffee, he said, "I advise all my patients of their diagnosis; some accept it with stoic calmness, but I know their mind is in turmoil". I felt this comment was directed at myself and so I responded, "My turmoil is past. The findings are an immeasurable relief". I then shared with him the awareness I had of my condition and how that came about. I explained why I believed my cancer would never shorten my life, though it could be the means God used to transport me from this world. The day of my death was appointed in the realms of Eternity. Nothing could efface that. Illness, I told him, was not necessary to His purpose though He often used it. I went on to illustrate how not one cell in my body could divide or multiply, normally or abnormally, except by His command. It was He, at His Will, who stayed or permitted the progression of disease, thus every cancerous cell in my body was under Divine Order. I told him about God's wondrous plan and how I thought of Him as Master Planner of my own life. Everything He did He pronounced 'very good'. This gracious man listened without interruption, finally saying, "I understand what you are saying, but it is not my philosophy". Quietly and in few words I tried to enable him to see how knowing the Lord would help him in his work when sharing unhappy news with patients and when trying to give them some measure of comfort. As we parted, arrangements for my admission to a mainland hospital finalised, he wished me well. I still think of him and pray that God will meet with him in a saving way.

Returning to work I shared the news of my impending hospitalisation with my immediate boss, advising him of the likelihood of my being off work for some weeks. I then attended a finance meeting, cleared my desk and drove home. Ahead lay unexplored terrain.

That evening I informed my helper Morag of the outcome of my visit to outpatients. She was taken aback by my news, but when she offered to accompany me to Inverness, I was absolutely delighted. The journey to hospital had been troubling me. I dreaded getting on and off the 'plane. As I pondered this on the way home I thought, "If I had family they would accompany me". Morag's suggestion was, in my eyes, God sent. I was relieved to the point of happiness. On Morag's part it was certainly a sacrifice. She had never flown before and she had to find cover for her work. But God ordered and she obeyed. My happiness was real for my God had not failed me at my first hurdle.

Actually, in the week leading up to hospitalisation I rested a lot. It was easier than moving around. Morag called each day and in the evening she would visit and lock the door from the outside taking the key with her. The Lord kept my mind so stayed upon Himself that this circumstance, which stemmed from my providence, did not disturb me. Amazingly I was kept from self-pity, not by anything in me, but by His Grace. I had plenty of time to think and as I lay in bed, my thoughts were taken up, not with bone scans and radiotherapy, but with Eternity. I recalled my mother's death and thought of the soul's separation from the body. How imperceptible the parting of spirit from matter! I thought of my own soul leaving my body; here (earth) and there (Eternity) in one gasp. Measuring, as we do, all things by time, it is natural to imagine this translation taking some fraction of time, but this is not so. It occurs instantly, simultaneous with that last breath. I then thought of the Holy Angels who hover around the death bed of the Saints, their presence ministering comfort and spiritual solace until finally they accompany the departed soul into the presence of the Father. But what of the fallen angels? We would like to forget them, yet they are there too, hoping that even in the throes of death, they may snatch the soul for their master. Conflict to the end! Praise God this cannot happen. None of His Children can ever be lost Eternally. For the believer facing death, this is tremendous assurance.

Reflecting thus, my meditation was led towards the intermediary phase - the phase between death and the resurrection of the body. I could readily identify with a Heaven of risen spiritual bodies, but a Heaven inhabited by disembodied spirits begged question. Not because I didn't believe it, but because my knowledge was so limited. Thus I questioned, "did Spirit recognise Spirit in Eternity, and if so how?" Again, it was easy to believe that in our risen bodies we would see and recognise. But the essence of Spirit defied my understanding. My debate continued. "What", I wanted to know, "were the activities of the Spirits in Eternity?" I thought of all the departed believers from the beginning of time. This added up to a lot of Spirits, but Spirit did not require space. Must I adjust my thinking in relation to Heaven? In conversation and singing we often refer to the Saints? Could a Saint be soul only? 'Together let my Saints unto me gathered be'. My mind had pictured sanctified soul and glorified body. We read, '.... his Saint's souls keepeth He ....'. What did this indicate? Perhaps my perception was wrong? I once read that, 'God sometimes puts His children to bed in the dark'. This amply summed up the way I felt. But I had to trust when I could not understand and so I began to think thoughts of Heaven, as it was known to me through His Word. A place flooded with His Glory, where the souls of believers lived in rapturous state, singing the Song of Moses and the Lamb, triumphant and clothed in robes made white in the blood of the Lamb. My thoughts at this point were 'most sweet' as they delighted in the glories of the Saints' inheritance. But I did not graze in these pastures for long. Overawed, by the wonderment of it all I thought of God, a Being without beginning and without end. A Triune God whom the world, the heaven of heavens and the Heavenly places could not contain. Inhabiting everywhere, all the time, at the same time. Never without existence. ......And then the thought came, "what if God doesn't exist?"

I had floundered on this rock before. Now my mind, as at other times, met a vacuum. Satan's cunning did not confine itself to the garden of Eden, at this moment he was filling my mind with disbelief. Just as Eve listened, so did I. "How can you be sure of what lies beyond time?". Oh! the subtlety of the questioner. This could have occupied my thoughts to my spiritual detriment, only it did not. I knew deep in my soul the answer and I believed. Was this, I wondered, what was meant by being, 'Plunged in the Godhead's deepest sea, And lost in His immensity'. For I certainly was. I returned to the Rock of my faith. The just must live by it, not by unanswerable and undeterminable questions. It was a strange going forth of thought, but I could not say it was spiritually unproductive for I was taught in it.

The evening before I left several friends called in after Church. Their reaction could be seen in their faces. Each shook hands solemnly and asked me how I was. "I'm very well", I said, "and I am going to enjoy every minute of the fellowship this evening". I cannot imagine what they thought but I am sure my response was not what was expected. Someone with cancer, going for treatment and declaring she was, 'very well' did not make sense. But we had a wonderful evening and everyone enjoyed it. To me it was special, a royal evening, honoured by the presence of the King of Glory.

Next morning a few friends came to see me off, each feeling sad on account of my cancer, while I could only feel happy. To the outsider I would have seemed at least naive, at most unwise. My disposition came from the Lord Himself otherwise it could not be sustained. In this I have often acknowledged, through the years, the Lord's goodness. If I were overly concerned for myself, morbid or neurotic, life would be difficult to live alone. But my Lord who gave me my providence, gave me with my cancer and my aloneness Grace and an attitude towards the disease which allows me to think and speak of it without ever feeling cast down.

'O, that men to the Lord would give,
Praise for His goodness still'.

With His goodness sustaining me, I set off on the next step of the journey.

chapter fourteen

Radiotherapy

'Without striking the iron how can it become a tool?'

The 'plane soars heavenward and I journey into the unknown ... but do I? God has commanded this journey, a God to whom everything is known, who did not just design the treatment plan which is to be the course of action, but manages it as well. He is the God who is my refuge, my strength, my present aid and who energises my will. He is the God who is fashioning the iron that it may become a tool fit for His own use. He is the God of direction, the unparalleled teacher, the trusted friend. 'Deep calleth unto deep'; the waves of my heart called out to the Great Deep which is Himself for I knew that as the 'plane would descend into the clouds, ultimately to meet the ground, so I would find myself, from time to time, in the clouds and grounded.

'They mount to Heaven, then to the depths
They do go down again'.

In this too-ing and fro-ing the Lord never loses sight of His Children, though they often lose sight of Him. His ties with them are stronger than death. This is the Lord who 'measured the waters in the hollow of His hand, and meted out Heaven with the span, and comprehended the dust of the earth in a measure and weighed the mountains in scales, and the hills in a balance'. Amazing as it may seem this is the God who journeys with me, a God whose vastness none can comprehend. It is enough that He knows what lies ahead.

Perceiving that the taxi is drawing up at the hospital doors, I heave a nostalgic sigh. Soon I shall be parted from those who accompanied me thither. But this is not a time for nostalgia; it is a time for moving forward to meet the next stage of God's plan. It is eight months since my pain and I first met. By God's Grace and the means to be used, hopefully we will be parted, at least for a time. The writer of Ecclesiastes advises that there is a time for everything. This is my time, and with His help, it is a time for positive thought, not negative action.

Taking the lift to the appropriate level I momentarily experience, on reading the sign, 'Ward 2A - Radiotherapy', the same unreal feeling I had when my doctor first suggested metastasis. Was this really happening to me? Radiotherapy, what connotations it held! Now it was my portion and it emphasised that my cancer was on the move. Suddenly I felt very alone and very vulnerable, humanly speaking. My friends would soon return home; they could not walk this path with me. I was swamped by a feeling akin to homesickness, yet again, I cried unto my Lord; He heard and delivered me from all my fears. He was teaching me that, Peter-like, as soon as I would take my eyes from off Him I would sink.

Bone scans, X-rays and other investigative procedures are now over and I await the result. Waiting time is action time. How would I respond if the bone scan showed more than one lesion? I knew my early responses but the sufficiency of His Grace must envelop me all the time. Yesterday's Grace would not carry me through today's troubles. I did, what in the circumstances came naturally, I prayed for enabling Grace to accept whatever would unfold. I prayed that if my disease was widespread it would not come as a shock, that by His help I would receive it gladly as a furtherance of His gift. I prayed that I would conduct myself as a Christian, that I would speak as a Christian and that I would show a Christ-like spirit. Thus as I sat and waited, I prayed the same prayer over and over again.

Arriving with his team, the Consultant politely asked if he might sit down. "Please do", I responded. He went on, "Do you mind if my colleagues sit, they are on their feet all day". Assuring him that I did not, I reflected on his consideration of his team members. This was not in evidence in my clinical days. Extremely impressed by the consultant's graciousness I forgot his mission. His introduction was a manifestation of excellent psychology. But even more important was the fact that we were all seated and we were at eye level contact one with another. I have since used this as an example of good doctor/patient communication.

"Has your neck ever given you any problems", the Consultant enquires. I thought, "Aha! there must be something significant in that remark". I was soon to learn that bone scans can show up more than metastatic lesions and that 'hot spots' require follow up X-ray. As I had not had radiotherapy following mastectomy this was a new experience for me, but my many questions were responded to with refreshing openness. I felt reassured that I would continue to be told the full facts of the progress of my disease. As the Consultant took his leave, I had the intensest feeling of thankfulness. The Lord was in control. His love cast out fear.

My walking difficulties necessitated the use of a wheelchair to and from the radiotherapy department. This was a relief rather than a vexation of spirit. I was occupied by everyone's legs as we made our way along the corridor. Would I ever walk again as freely and as painlessly as those I observed? I wondered if they realised the privilege which was theirs. Then I thought, "Had I?" I knew the answer. Every privilege is accepted as a right until God intervenes. I felt no envy towards them. They had their cross, as I had mine. I felt content.

I spoke with the porters who wheeled me along day by day. They may well be in Eternity before myself, but I felt they did not expect to be. I wondered if they felt sorry for me and thankful on their own account. I was certain they did. Radiotherapy bespoke to them my disease and I felt that in their eyes my days were numbered. How foolish we can be in our thinking, but then cancer continues to have an iron grip over the minds of many.

The approach to the radiotherapy room was interesting. It was a long-angled corridor off the main corridor, with the distinctive radiation warning signs in black on yellow positioned at the entrance and painted on the doors, in itself a reminder that this was no ordinary treatment. The therapy room was spacious but, again, the thick walls, the absence of windows to the outside, the robust looking lead lined doors and the protected equipment bespoke the fact that radiation was potentially dangerous and that the only reason I was about to be subjected to it was the fact that I had cancer.

I had previously been advised that I required ten treatments. The process was now explained to me in detail and questions invited. My skin had already been indelibly marked. This ensured that the emission of rays would be directed each day to the same area. Healthy as well as cancerous cells can be destroyed by radiation and these markings were very important. The couch on which I was required to lie was located beneath a very large unconventional machine. Staff positioned both me and it until the area to be treated was in direct line with the beam. Instructing me to remain very still, they withdrew from the room, closing the doors fast. Soft music began to play and the machine, switched on from outwith the room, whined away. Through the small leaded glass window, just above their computer equipment, staff observed their patient.

Aware of the length of my treatment and concerned that I might imperceptibly alter my position I began to count, each number accounting for one second. After the given time the machine switched off and staff re-entered the room. Amazed by this immediacy I was told the process was like a microwave oven. The instant it switched off it was safe to open the door. While talking with me staff were re-positioning. The machine was swung so that the beam was now beneath the couch. The delivery of radiation could thus attack the tumour from back to front as well as from front to back. The series recommenced.

This time I reflected on radiation. Its silent power amazed me. I imagined those carefully calculated doses hitting my cancerous cells as they instantly beamed through the couch on which I lay and through the bony tumour hidden in my body. I was overwhelmed by the fact that the Lord when He created earth, placed within its bosom, as a natural substance, that which would, in time, alleviate certain of mankind's ailments - and man not yet created. Here I lay, benefitting from this very substance because my Lord had planned it for me before He even created the earth and planted it therein. I believed these rays, under His Divine authority would relieve my condition and as the days passed my thoughts continued to focus on this as I prayed, "Lord, if it be Thy Will may these rays ease my pain, and if not bestow Thy Grace so that I might accept whatsoever unfolds from Thy plan".

A patient's inner response to radiotherapy is something I neither read of nor heard discussed, but I am sure I am not unique in the feelings it provoked within myself. In its application radiotherapy is absolutely painless yet I was aware of something which is incredibly difficult to describe. It was not fear or anxiety, I felt neither, but each time the machine whined - when operative it makes a whining noise - I was aware of an uncanny almost eerie sensation. Was it the whine, the unnatural environment, the solitary confinement, the isolation from all human contact, the mysterious transmission of radiation or the similarities with dying, which also must be experienced alone and bereft of loved ones, I cannot tell. I only know that though these sensations were fleeting I was able to identify them. They were in no way disconcerting, neither did they disturb my communion with my Lord. I always believed that He was the authority behind my radio-therapy and this remained unaffected while the perception of my senses received these impressions.

Back on the ward I recalled training days in Glasgow. I had never worked in the radiotherapy unit, but I had nursed patients receiving 'radium', as we then called it. This treatment was much less refined and sophisticated than we know it today, but what clung to my mind was the effect skin markings had on us young nurses. Patients not long admitted would go down to the Unit and return with these black skin markings. They were only ever seen on patients with cancer. The association provoked within us a hostility towards the disease so that we would rather forget it than face it. Studies have shown that nurses' stress levels increase as they identify with cancer patients and in particular breast cancer. But He never gives a superfluous experience and these feelings of long ago, now awakened, taught me to remember those attending to myself. I shared with them my experience, trying to put the disease in perspective and always seeking to give God the Glory and to show what He can do when we trust in Him. Had someone in those far off days told me I would be the bearer of these very marks from which I then cringed I would have recoiled. Had someone said my cancer would occur thirty years later, I might have relaxed. This was a lifetime away. Had someone said I would be delighted to be the bearer of this disease, seeing it as a precious gift from Him, I would have concluded I had taken leave of my senses. But this is what God does. With the affliction He gives Himself and through the sufficiency of His Grace in the time of our need, the desert in our lives 'shall rejoice and blossom as the rose' and 'our time of suffering will be a time of love'.

chapter fifteen

Sensitive Issues

---

*'He that dwelleth in the secret place of the Most High
shall abide under the shadow of the Almighty'.*

"You realise cancer is not curable", the Consultant went on to say. "Yes", I replied. He paused, "If you were to ask me, how long?" "I wouldn't ask that", I interjected. Without appearing to hear me, he said, "About five years, in the meantime you may return to work, full or part time". This was my final consultation prior to discharge the following morning. I thanked him sincerely for all he had done for me and with a brief greeting we parted.

Did his words discourage me? Not at all. The All-Wise God purposeth, I firmly believe this. We are not promised life even for the duration of one breath, let alone five years. From long experience with given diseases, doctors may predict reasonably accurately, but my mind was stayed on my Lord and I just said to myself, "Only the Lord knows how long". It felt as though I had been told nothing. Of much more concern was the degree of pain I still experienced. In my ignorance I had expected relief from my first radiotherapy treatment. It had never crossed my mind that I should require assistance on my return flight home. Thus, as the plane taxied to a standstill, I pondered how I was to negotiate the steps. For some reason the need for the bone to ossify (repair itself) had never occurred to me, despite my awareness of bone destruction by cancer and subsequently by radiation. I thought of the poem,

> '*All God's angels come to us disguised*
> *Sorrow, sickness, pain and death .....'*

Pain, an angel? Why not? Pain had already been a precursor to His presence and His joy in my life, a messenger which showed the mysteries of circumstances which passed human explanation.

It was almost four months before the pain receded to the point of forgetfulness, during which, the words of another seemed appropriate, "Give me patience to endure this pain which Thou seest fit I should suffer, so that it may be sanctified unto me and I may find in it the blessing which all Thy gifts contain". I had always seen my cancer as a gift from His Hand and my pain as an associate of this gift. I had never heard anyone speak of cancer thus and I had never, until now, read of pain as a gift. I began to deliberate as to whether pain was one gift and cancer another, but I concluded that, in my case, they were inseparable components of the same gift. How much easier providence can be borne when His Hand is seen in it from beginning to end. As I looked back I thought, "how fitting His gift", and how wonderful to be led, in the furnace of pain, by the quiet waters. For this is how it seemed, a 'Come ye apart' experience, during which I was enabled to concentrate my mind on reading, especially material relating to Heaven, I seemed to have an insatiable thirst to know more about the 'City .... whose builder and maker is God'.

No experience continues forever. We read that after the Transfiguration there was the foot of the mount experience. Thus it was in my case, while my soul magnified my Lord as I returned to health and to work, so the frailties of my nature and the distractions of my mind pressed upon me, until I began to sense a cooling of my spiritual ardour. The trappings of worldly endeavour and of daily living, in themselves quite legitimate, together with an obstinate heart were soon to weigh heavily upon me. Work was often a high pressure scenario and tiredness a by-product so that I was unable to devote time to spiritual matters as I had done when I was laid aside. I mourned over my failings, realising His need to apply the chastening rod over and over again. Yet, I took courage from His wonderful faithfulness and from the fact that, 'His compassions fail not'.

At this time the words of St. Augustine seemed to reflect my thoughts. 'Narrow is the mansion of my soul, enlarge Thou it that Thou may'st enter in. It is ruinous, repair Thou it'. I began to consider the authors I browsed through, Whitefield, Spurgeon, Rutherford, McCheyne and others. They were so consistent in their lives, so dedicated in their labours for their Lord, so urgent in their prayers and so disciplined in their Christian walk. I questioned how they achieved this and concluded their steadfastness arose from their nearness to their Lord. I, many times, purposed to discipline my life but on each occasion failed miserably. These men had no use for the worldliness of thought and living which affected my life to the leanness of my soul. "Lord, help me", I prayed, "to turn from the folly of my ways to the Fountain of Life and help me to praise Thee for the administrations of Thy grace".

During these months I was faced with the sensitive issue of divine healing. Friends outwith the Island, who are very dear to me and I to them, longed for me to be free from disease. Cautiously they suggested healing through prayer, enquiring at the same time as to my views on divine healing. Had I ever considered it? I never had. Indeed I had a complete antipathy to it. I stood firm in my belief that the Lord could heal me, if He so chose, without my ever seeking the laying on of hands or any form of divine healing. In the same way as I brought all my other problems to Him I brought my ill health. According to His Will and His Divine Power He could heal; He had but to speak the word. I had no need to authorise external agencies; my faith in Him was absolute.

Confronted with this theme over a period of time, I wondered why the Lord's people should have such an urgent need to be healed. After all He could use His infirm children equally effectively as instruments of His power. Why the lack of contentment? Disease was but the outworking of His Will and something which He alone controlled and which merited our Amen. I was mystified how those so bent on healing could not grasp the sublimity of His dealings, after all ill-health is often a means through which the Lord sanctifies His children. Might it not, therefore, be more profitable to accept His providence as He willed and gifted?

One evening in a friend's home, following a discussion on this subject, I began to think seriously of what was said. I questioned as to whether I might like to be healed and laying aside all counter arguments, I concluded that any such desire I might have was selfishly motivated and, therefore, not God glorifying. Next morning some visitors called, one of whom I had never met. He was a retired minister whose wife had died of cancer three months previously. When I enquired after the health of one of the party who had been unwell, she replied, "I have just disgraced the family by attending a divine healing service". I thought to myself, "Is there no getting away from this subject?" As they left, her brother, the person I had never hitherto met, turned to me and said, "Don't you seek divine healing. If God wishes to heal you He will do so without laying on of hands". He fortified my own point of view. He then handed me a small pamphlet which he had written at the time of his wife's illness. On it he wrote two texts which were of considerable comfort to his wife in the terminal phase and expressed a hope they might be of like comfort to me.

Our meeting was not by our choice. God organised it and through it He confirmed to me that my thoughts on this subject were in harmony with His Will. This minister had no intention of breaking his journey midway, but he was persuaded so to do. He was returning from a preaching engagement in Aberdeen en route to Edinburgh where he was to catch a train to his home city in England. God's timing is perfect.

This was not the end of the matter. I was later to observe, while on holiday, quite without realising that it was to be part of the evening ministry, a session of prayer for healing. The leader invited any present who wished prayer for this purpose to come forward. Many did and many others came forward to pray with them. As an on-looker I found it a most uncomfortable and confusing service. Each person prayed for was held in the arms of the person who prayed. Everyone prayed out aloud and at the same time. There was no felt Presence, no real reverence, indeed it was quite cold, clinical and vague. I couldn't believe anyone would be healed as a consequence. In fact, I doubted whether those prayed for would ever again be remembered after the holiday was over. Perhaps I should seek forgiveness for my scepticism and unbelieving heart.

This issue was to rear its head again through an advertisement for a video, the sleeve caption of which read,'Meeting X could change your life'. It was the story of a woman who had breast cancer and claimed she had been healed. Obeying an irresistible prompting I wrote the publishers, firstly, drawing their attention to the fact that only the Lord can change lives and secondly, challenging the claim to healing. Such assertions are very confusing and often not very consistent. It begs the question, what is healing? Some would respond, the total eradication of disease. But how is this known? Many diseases, cancers included, go into remission, sometimes, as in my own case, for lengthy periods. Healing should have permanency, remission does not. There can be nothing more devastating for the individual and his or her family than to believe healing has occurred, only to discover some time later a secondary tumour. What about the Lord's cause in such circumstances, might it not suffer a set-back? It is surely unwise for us frail creatures, with understandings so marred by sin, to make such profound claims, unless absolute Divine Authority has spoken it. Even then, spiritual discernment is necessary.

On this issue, my thoughts became entrenched. I reasoned thus. When I cut my finger I feel it; a dressing is applied and it usually heals by 'first intention'. Who affords me the healing propensity of my immune system? Surely my Maker. By the same token, when I have cancer in my bones, I feel it; radiation is applied and the bone heals. Wherein lies the difference? We are unconcerned about the cut finger but feel a need for 'healing' following the treatment of cancer. Does this really make sense? A cut finger could end in septicaemia. If God decreed, septicaemia could end in death, just the same outcome as that of the cancer we so much dread. It could be the same outcome with any disease, even the common cold, if God so wished. In everything God purposeth. He is Sovereign, He is the supreme power. There is no escaping the cup of suffering and it is prudent to face it and accept it, knowing that He will do as seemeth Him good, always to His Glory, always to His Children's spiritual betterment. The wise man leaves all to Him and to the totality of His power.

This subject does not conclude the sensitive issues which may be met with. What about the media attention received by some celebrities when it is perceived that they suffer from cancer? Feature upon feature is written. We read about their courage, about the way in which they fight their disease, of their spirit of determination to overcome their condition and so on. Is this intended to convey an undaunted spirit or is it a striving to master the cancer power-struggle in their bodies? If so, it has a hollow ring which saddens the heart.

A few years ago I received several instalments of a serialised book which was written by a well known person who developed cancer. Across the top of the page of the first instalment was a reference to the author's courage. Overcome by the excesses of the language and a feeling of hopelessness, I could only read two instalments. Perhaps the feelings evoked are discernible in the following letter. The letter is abridged and certain minor alterations effected to take account of this.

Dear ....

I have just received the first instalment of your serialised autobiography and I feel compelled to respond to you in writing. Far from being encouraged, I feel deeply saddened. In common with many other readers I found some of the language highly offensive and the general tenor of the serial without hope.

Hundreds of women have had cancers and hundreds more breast cancer. Some know of their condition and their prognosis, some do not. Some do not want to, in case their fears are confirmed. Yet, each has her own testimony, each an experience and each could write almost an identical account of the happenings. Some take courage from reading about the experiences of other cancer sufferers, some cannot bear to be reminded of what they went through, some accept it, some bury their heads ostrich-like and some others, like the unaffected public, prefer not to be reminded of the possibilities of contracting it.

Basically, women are not so very different. They may have differing coping mechanisms and differing threshold levels of endurance, but their responses are very much the same. They struggle with varying degrees of emotional fears, anxieties and the inevitable sleepless nights, as they try to come to terms with what the majority find a devastating situation. But this is normal to all.

Many books have been written by mastectomy patients. One author has written, to my knowledge, three books on the subject. She has been involved with broadcasts and appeared on television. Such books and associated writings find their way to me and what strikes me is their absolute sameness. Read one history and you have read them all. Could it be that the authors have a need to recount and record these facts as a means of therapy, to reassure themselves? It surely can't be egotistical?

I have met and I had close contact with very many cancer patients in my day, including four members of my family who are now deceased, and I have had the opportunity to listen, comfort and encourage many more. I have read about cancer, attended seminars in connection with it and given talks on it. Furthermore, I had a mastectomy in 1979 and a metastic lesion diagnosed in April 1988. I have had all the usual X-rays, mammography, bone scans and radiotherapy. I think, therefore, I am reasonably qualified to respond to your article.

Why does it sadden me? Because it offers no hope, it puts its trust in a service and in the individuals responses. I mentioned earlier that our basic instincts are not very different, but our outlook, attitudes and the degree to which our spirits plummet or soar can differ enormously. Our personalities cannot be discounted.

Before acknowledging credit for a resigned attitude towards the disease, one's condition must be put into perspective. When that intrusive lump is found, the person concerned is usually in good health. This differs significantly from sufferers of some internal cancers. Why, therefore, is this particular group described as courageous? There are many diseases more disabling, more disfiguring and more tragic than cancer. For instance, if I had taken a stroke I might be unable to communicate or to write and I might have partial paralysis. I certainly could not continue in my job. How would society view me? Probably as an individual unable to perform as a useful citizen? My sense of values would no longer be obvious. Would I be classified as courageous? Sadly not.

I went to a meeting in extreme pain, after my diagnosis was confirmed. I went home in the evening, cooked a meal as best I could and among other things read the newspaper. Was I brave or courageous? Not at all. I was simply in a state of resignation.

Cardio vascular disease heads the mortality rate and yet, there is no public sympathy or admiration given to this group and very few books or articles are penned by them. Unfortunately, cancer breeds dread in the minds of many; it is synonymous with death and this is chilling, therefore, living with it must be courageous. But is this really so?

If I were to share with you what cancer did for me, the very positive dimension it has added to my life, so that I would not wish to have missed the experience, how would you respond? I have been led to think through the terminal phase of my illness, the fatigue, the listlessness, the loss of appetite, without morbid or melancholy feelings or being in any way depressed.

A secondary lesion brings with it a realisation that spread has occurred. There are fewer pegs upon which to hang one's hopes. Death is much more realistic, dying on the horizon of one's thoughts. The summit of life is reached, the descent into the Valley commenced. Whether the journey be short and sharp or long and tortuous is not known, but the Lord knows and that is all that matters.

Why this euphoria during the two episodes of my cancer? Because Someone came close to me and I leaned hard upon Him and He gave me songs in the dark nights of my experience. He has a wise plan for my life, a plan written in eternal love. He promises that the day of my death will be more blessed than the day of my birth. He has shown me what He has prepared for His children and He has promised to be with me. The union begun here on earth between Christ and His Church is to be consummated in Heaven. Herein is hope, my hope and what zest this spiritual dimension has added to my life! Living or dying - His. What He has done for me He can do for you.

> With fellow feeling.
> Yours sincerely.

The brief reply indicated that many had been helped by her book and that there were different ways of coping. She had hers, I had mine. The reply assured me she had at least read the letter and I often remembered her, hoping that God would use something therein to speak to her of her soul before her demise. I have no knowledge of the remainder of her life, but the period after her primary cancer was, I understand, not very long. The recollection fills me with sadness, even as I write. How different from recollecting the journey of the Lord's children. It is so positive.

Following this incident I had a distinct aversion to material written by cancer sufferers and in particular those who wrote of breast cancer. I would never buy such books, nor pay much attention to those which came to hand. Even Christian authors disappointed. Thus the promptings over many years of well meaning colleagues and friends, some now in Glory, to place my own account in writing, fell on deaf ears. My resolve hardened and I refused to put pen to paper. That I should do so now is a complete mystery and a miracle, even to myself. I have to believe the Lord is behind it; the purpose, unknown to me, will unfold either in time or in Eternity.

chapter sixteen

Marching Orders

'Then trust Me and fear not; thy life is secure,
My wisdom is perfect, supreme is My power'.

The train edged slowly out of Haymarket Station. At the next stop all remaining passengers would alight. As the train advanced through the tunnel and out into the open again my attention, as always, was arrested by the jagged, overhanging, volcanic rock which loomed ahead as if defiantly warding off attack; on its top, perched precariously, stood the famous Edinburgh Castle. It had dominated the City for centuries and had attracted and intrigued millions of visitors from all over the world, intent on seeing its mysteries and the Crown Jewels housed therein or, if the timing was appropriate, the renowned tattoo.

My eyes took in the scene on the opposite side of the train. There was Princes Street, with its milling crowds and its tartan and woollen shops. It had a grandeur all of its own. Sedate gardens, stretching the length of the street, attracted weary, harassed shoppers and visitors alike. Revitalised by the sheer beauty of the gardens, by the song of the birds in the trees and the wonder of the architecture of the commemorative statues, they would move on refreshed. Yes, I thought, a truly regal City. But the train was grinding to a halt and with head down I hastened from the station towards St. Andrew's House, there to meet with colleagues and to address the pressing issues of the Health Service as these affected nursing.

On my return to my hotel at the end of the day my thoughts suddenly swept over the events of the meeting I had attended in Lewis the previous evening. The project was now well under way and the Committee were at the stage of agreeing and ordering furnishings. It was rather exciting, especially as I had been associated with it, in one form or another, since its inception. With the General Manager of the Health Board I had met the Chairman and members of the small sub-committee representing the Presbytery, at their first and subsequent meetings. Their mission was to find a way by which they could assist in supplementing and complementing the Health Service locally. It was during these meetings that the idea of the Island's first voluntary nursing home and hospice was crystallised. The Committee had come a long way since these early visionary days, when their faith was so often tried; now the complex was almost a reality.

As I entered the foyer of the hotel I tried to visualize all the items chosen, in their formal setting. I worried a little; would the curtains, carpets, soft and hard furnishings blend in with each other and with the wall decor? Quite without realising where my thoughts were leading I found myself wondering what it would be like to work there? Despite my involvement, first as a member of the main committee and latterly as a co-opted member of the furnishings sub-committee, I had never thought through the actual implications of working there or the practical issues of setting up the service. I expected my involvement to cease with commissioning and these aspects would be dealt with by whomsoever was ultimately appointed as Matron. Now, as the evening progressed I mulled over this and while my thoughts wandered hither and thither they did not produce effective outgoings. In fact, I dismissed them. To work there required that I resign from my post with the Health Service. This was contrary to my intentions. I had a good job, but the greatest hurdle was my health. I had never thought of retirement, early or otherwise; I just concluded I would continue working as long as my health permitted. Another post?, I couldn't entertain it. With hindsight, the working out of these thoughts were the beginnings of God's marching orders to me.

Back at my desk, these thoughts were soon set aside, that is, until I went to Keswick, with friends, for the holiday week of the convention.

In the large tent the missionary was recounting her experiences. "You are never too old to do something for the Lord", she told the audience, as she touched on her own call to Africa. In Keswick, five years previously, she heard God speak to her. She said to her husband as the service ended "The Lord has just called me to Africa". "Go", he said. "He hasn't called me but I will support you from the homeland". Big-hearted, yes, but when God is in a thing He will remove all obstacles so that His plan can be effected. Nothing exceptional about this except, perhaps, that the lady in question was sixty years old at the time. Now, five years later, having been to Africa and written a book about her work there, she was addressing the convention.

As I sat and listened, a single soul among the thousands present, my heart was strongly moved. All the previous stirrings of thirty eight years ago flooded back. I took stock of my life and concluded I had never done anything positive for my Lord. What could I now do? Fifty four years of age and suffering from cancer, it seemed impossible. Could I go abroad? What could I do there? Clinical work was out of the question. I felt in a real spiritual quandary. "Lord", I prayed, tears coursing down my cheeks, "use me, however long or short a time I may have to live". It was genuine prayer, and through the gloom of my spirit I became aware of a positive response deep in my being. If God, I reasoned, wants me to do something specific for Him, cancer will not stand in His way. Age will not stand in His way. Cancer is such a simple thing to Him, I knew it could in no way deter His plan. Even in my own eyes it became insignificant.

Moving out of the tent I became aware that my friend's husband was also affected. Without either of us being aware of it at the time, for they reside on the mainland, we were both to retire from our separate employments on the same day, he to enter the ministry. But I am going ahead of my story.

I returned from holiday, but work was never the same again. Day by day I felt I was being weaned away from it. About six months later I began to entertain thoughts of early retirement. God was now giving His marching orders. Corrie Ten Boom used to say, "Don't bother to give God instructions, just report for duty". I hadn't learned this yet.

My secretary had been on prolonged leave and the morning she returned I shared with her my thoughts of retirement. She seemed somewhat taken aback. I was several years from normal retiring age and like everyone else in the organisation, she had never envisaged this as a possibility. Her surprise was nothing to the shock which awaited her after lunch. When God is at work anything can happen. His timing is not ours. I had never positively vocalised my thoughts up until that morning. If I had I am sure my friends would have tried to dissuade me. As I partook of my simple office lunch I questioned what, if anything, was preventing me from effecting my decision. I had never questioned this before. Was it loss of status, of money or simply insecurity? I was still in good health, at least I was feeling well. How would I channel my energies if I retired? What would I do? With astonishing suddenness I came to my decision. I crossed over to my desk, wrote out my letter of resignation, walked along the corridor and handed it to an astonished General Manager. By the time my secretary was back from lunch I had started working my notice. My spirit felt incredibly free. God's final marching orders were swift.

Immediately my decision was known I was faced with the issue of retiring on the grounds of ill health. Well-meaning and kindly colleagues tried to persuade me, knowing the advantages this held for me. They never could understand my reaction, in fact, some were of the view that I was being a bit obtuse. Other Christians had done it, I was told, why couldn't I? In this, my resolve was firm. For me it would be wrong and unethical. I knew my medical history afforded me the opportunity but my Lord had given me the health to undertake a demanding job and my cancer had not prevented me from fulfilling my contract. In fact I felt very well. Could I use my health to enhance my financial position? Certainly not. I was convinced I was right in the stand I was taking. Many who spoke with me were unbelievers and I was of the view He permitted this trial, for this is what I found it to be, to afford me the opportunity to witness on His behalf. It was an opportunity I might not otherwise have had. 'Him that honoureth me I will honour'. I was to see this fulfilled.

Leaving the Health Service had its poignancy. It was the end of an era which lasted thirty seven years and how quickly they had passed.

At home that evening, alone, and surrounded by all the gifts of well wishers I sat down and thought "What have I done?" Have I taken the right decision? The Lord did not leave me long in this frame of mind. He sent someone with whom I was able to share Christian experience and the feeling of that moment passed for ever. A day or two later, as I stood at the kitchen sink, I was overcome by a desire to do something for my Lord. "Help me", I prayed, "to do something for Thee before I leave this earth. Whatever remains of my life, take it and use it". It was as if my Keswick experience was being renewed.

I thoroughly enjoyed my brief retirement. It was the time of the autumn communion season and I hardly missed a weekend without being at some communion. The fellowship I really appreciated. I could relax and enjoy it without an awareness of working on Monday mornings. But Satan hadn't retired; he was insidiously employing his machinations and it took me some time before I recognised this. I would breakfast and light the fire and then something would say to me, "do this and that before you sit down for worship and you will be more relaxed". Instead of beginning the day with Him I found, on occasions, it was lunchtime before I opened the Word. I was out of the routine I had when working and instead of having more time to spend in devotions it appeared as though I was so busy I had less. 'Hours for the world, moments for Christ', someone once said. How true. Satan is a lot cleverer than we think.

Two and a half months later the post of Matron for Bethesda, the project spoken of, was advertised. To some it was a foregone conclusion that I would apply. This was certainly not so. I questioned myself as to whether I should. What did the Lord want me to do? To be face to face with a decision was a very different proposition to the thoughts of a year previously in my hotel in Edinburgh. I knew I had the skills to do the job and the ability to promote the service. I also had many contacts but this wasn't enough. I needed to know definitely that He was with me and that any promptings I might have were from Himself. In the end I did apply and as I waited on the Lord in prayer the morning of my interview, the words which spoke to me were, 'Who is sufficient for these things'. Was I? I certainly didn't feel that I was. Instead I had an enormous burden. What was I letting myself in for? I was enjoying retirement, yet I had to let my name go forward. I knew it was right. The conviction was there. This is what the Lord would have me do. On the first of November 1991 I was back in harness.

What an incredible time, those early beginnings. The hand-over of the building was scheduled for the following February. In the meantime I, with a part-time secretary, started work in a small, cold, derelict room which was offered to us without rental costs. From here all the necessary documentation was processed and staff interviews organised and outstanding equipment ordered, received and checked. Our first staff appointment was at Sister level and she joined me in January 1992. Many a day, until the Unit was functional, she must have wondered what on earth she let herself in for as she compared her well organised and busy surgical ward with the bowels of some box into which she had disappeared as she tried to check orders. These were extraordinary months, exciting and very fulfilling, but for me there were personal concerns as well. As I visited the site and walked from room to room, a persistent gnawing pain reminded me of the seed of disease in my body. It forced me to consider the wisdom of applying for the post. Would I let everybody down? Would I ever see the commissioning through? These ever present thoughts compelled me, time and time again, to cast myself at the feet of the Master. I knew He was, as always, in control. I believed He had placed me in this post and I reminded myself that not one cancer cell would interfere with His plan. Thus I took courage in His sustaining Grace and from the fact that I believed the work was His. 'Who is sufficient for these things?'. I was to ask myself this again and again. Who indeed? The work seemed so great, my ability and my spiritual strength so weak, my health so precarious, but I believed that with His help I would see the work of commissioning through. I did. On the 9th of March 1992, I was to welcome our first residents to the nursing home and a week later our first patients to the hospice. One single word expresses my feelings and my praise. Hallelujah!

Nothing can surpass His wisdom. Six weeks into the operational workings of our complex and I was referred for a bone scan. Was my cancer on the move? This would soon be clear. In the words of Scripture,'What meaneth this? . Thinking of the short time I held office,

I and others, might well have asked the same question, except that I was at peace with His will.

'Faith must obey the Saviour's Will
As well as trust His Grace'.

chapter seventeen

A Further Episode

*'There is a hemisphere of the world in the sunshine
of work, there is another in the shadow of suffering'.*

I returned to the Department of Physics at the appointed time, my radio-active injection well dispersed throughout my body and the required quantity of fluid consumed. Familiarity with my surroundings lessened natural curiosity and allayed anxiety. For the next forty five minutes the physicist in charge of my scan would be captive audience. As I lay on the couch with yet another large machine gazing down on my frame, this one by now user-friendly, the Doctor of Physics would sit before his computer, arising from time to time to move the machinery as appropriate.

Depending upon whether or not I had met him previously, I would share with him, either the great things God had done for me since my last visit and how He and I and cancer were in unison because it had been blessed to me, or I would assure him that hosting cancer in my body was like sharing a home with a friend, and friends do not incite fear. I would explain the reason why this was so, that the Great Host Himself carries both me and it, making it an extraordinary blessing and a burden which is ever so light.

My calm unconcern amazes me at times. Even to myself it seems almost unnatural, such as on the occasion of which I write. I went for that scan, for the result and for the subsequent treatment with uncommon placidity. It must be attributed to the One whose name is Peace, for I am as human as everyone else and what is happening to me and in me is indicative of this. I am sure these professionals must sometimes think they are treating a simpleton!

When my condition dictates a visit to the department to which I refer, I view it as a mission. This is why I use my cancer to characterise and give impetus to what I really want to say. I have never met anyone totally unaffected by cancer. They are either concerned for themselves or their loved ones or the condition reminds them of some deceased relative. Everyone, professional or otherwise, has had some experience of it, if not in their own lives then in the lives of someone known to them. This creates within them a deep reverence towards the condition and those afflicted by it, which some see as a living death sentence.

Having come to see my own cancer as something positive which God has given me to use in His service, for as long as He leaves me on earth, I cannot keep quiet when opportunity presents. Perhaps it might seem unfair to share my reasoning, and what God can do, with professionals who, whatever their belief, cannot walk away from their patient or enter into argument. It would trouble me greatly if I did not. Perhaps someday they may have the same condition and I trust if they do they will recall the quaint middle-aged woman from Lewis who dominated their space in the scan room with supernatural reasoning and that the remembrance, by God's grace, will give them hope.

Scanning has always commenced, in my case, at about knee level, moving slowly upwards. Before the machine is positioned to obtain a lateral skeletal view, the upper frontal quadrant, shoulders, neck and head, is screened. During this process the machine is literally inches away from the face and because it is difficult to look into a solid metal plate which obscures the light I find it easier to close my eyes. I just lie quietly and think. Sometimes I wonder what the screen is telling the Doctor of Physics sitting beside me. Are there questionable 'hot spots'? It is the Consultant's responsibility to share the findings with the patient and so I resist the temptation of sounding him out.

Time passes very quickly, at least that is my experience, and soon the scan is over. This is normally undertaken fully clothed but on the occasion to which I now refer I had worn a blouse with metal buttons and I was required to remove it. Now, as I put it back on, the Truth speaks to me. I recognise it as Psalm eighteen. It has not spoken to me for very many years.

'And by my God assisting me
I overleap a wall'.

I believe the Lord is graciously preparing me, that my bone scan has shown up something which will be confirmed on X-ray. I feel no reaction as I thank my Lord for remembering me, only quiet resignation. The Physicist accompanies me to the X-ray department and as I thank him he says, "See you, anon". Yes, he expects me to return to his department at some time in the future. After all, time has proven that we all do. As the disease progresses this becomes the pattern of our lives. The Doctor has seen it all before. As I watch him walk back along the corridor I think, how little expectancy he has of the occurrence of ill health in his own life. The routine which becomes so much part of the cancer-patient's life is not one the healthy expect to have to undergo. Their kindly sympathy makes no allusion to their own vulnerability. Cancer patients often develop sensitive responses which heightens their intuitive perception. These would be found to be incredibly accurate if carers and others would but share with honesty their reactions.

As arranged I saw the Consultant that afternoon. "You have a slow growing tumour in your ischael tuberosity which has not shown any significant change since your previous scan but if you come in tomorrow I will arrange for you to have radiotherapy". Tomorrow! But I must get back. No-one knew I was away for a scan but Sister and I had several administrative matters to attend to. In addition I had not come prepared for admission. I shared my plight with a very understanding Consultant who made arrangements for the following Monday.

Back in Lewis I waited until Friday before I told my secretary. Having previously worked with me for four years in the Health Service, she had become as accustomed to these situations as I was myself. She showed little reaction. I wanted to attend the communions in a certain congregation that weekend without people clamouring around me and so I asked both Sister and herself not to disclose my news until after I was hospitalised. I decided to leave a note for staff so that they might learn of my condition from myself.

My pain, on this occasion, was much less acute. It was of a persistent, boring nature which became more marked as I walked and when I sat down I felt as if a small marble was on the chair. Nonetheless, it was relatively easy to live with and I could walk the long corridor to the radiotherapy department unaided. Feeling well, I arrived in hospital armed with recipe books and writing materials. Before Bethesda was operational I devised a four week menu rota with a choice of dish at each main meal. Not wishing these to become boring for long-term residents I always intended increasing the cycle by a further four weeks but time had not afforded the opportunity. I could now rectify this and utilise my time purposefully.

On each occasion hospitalised my condition was different but my responses were similar. I attribute this to my needs being met by my Lord out of His Riches in Glory. He sent many friends to visit, but one deserves special mention. He ministered in one of the town churches. Twice he called and each time he questioned me on my thoughts of death and the hereafter as these affected myself and then led the conversation from there. Within four weeks he was struck down with what proved to be his final illness. It was not cancer, but two months after we met in my hospital room, 'he was not, for God took him'. It puzzled me a great deal how I had not had the spiritual perception to recognise, either in our discussion or in his prayers, that God was ripening him for Glory. I certainly expected my home-call before his, but age and apparent health are irrelevant when He speaks.

On the last occasion on which we met he quoted a text from Corinthians on which he dwelt for a short while. Try as I might to recall it after he died I couldn't. One morning, months later, these words awoke me, 'But we all, with open face, beholding as in a glass the glory of the Lord, are changed into the same image from glory to glory even as by the Spirit of the Lord'. What could this mean? I hadn't been thinking of anything specific. Then like a flash something occurred to me. Was it possible that this was the text which was discussed in my hospital room?

The menus were by now complete and so I began writing to pass the time. These writings continued after I went home with no expectations of making further use of them, in fact, many were destroyed. From what has survived the following is an example of how I passed the time. Written in hospital, these thoughts come straight from the heart and if they are disjointed they are as they flowed into my mind.

Raigmore, April 1992

'And being in agony He prayed the more earnestly'.

'I have read these words many times, why have they arrested me on this occasion? How amazing that the King of Glory knew in His humanity what it was to be in agony. Agony - it bespeaks a painful experience, both mental and physical, one of extreme suffering, one of soul agony and this is what the Son of God required to endure on our behalf. How did He respond to this situation? How did he react? By praying the more earnestly. If He, our Lord, the Sinless, the Holy One, the perfect Son of God, the co-equal with the Father, the perfect Sacrifice, found Himself in a situation where He required to pray the more earnestly how much more we His creatures. Surely His example is encouragement for us to do likewise. Our agonies are minuscular by comparison and are tainted by our sinful nature. We get our deserts. He, Sinless One, did nothing to merit the path which He trod, the wine press - alone. No human being can enter into this, or into His human feelings, His human needs, His human responses as He went through His agony, His violent struggle. Alone? Yes. Alone, bereft of friends. Alone on the cross, forsaken of His Father.

'We can find ourselves in situations where we are bereft of friends and loved ones, of human empathy and human support, yet we are not alone, we will never be required to tread the wine press alone, we will never be forsaken of our Lord. We have a lifeline, access to the Father through the intercessory prayer of the Son and we have the Body of Christ, His Church, praying and interceding on our behalf. However low we become, we will never become as low as He did. We always have the everlasting arms beneath us. Oh! what our Lord suffered that we might have Eternal life. Our afflictions are indeed light.

'For our light affliction which is but for a moment worketh for us a far more exceeding and eternal weight of glory'.

This appropriate text accompanied a card I received just as these words were in the writing.

'Our afflictions were covenanted for our eternal good. They were planned by a caring, loving Father who will never leave us nor forsake us. They were planned for our good, planned for our sanctification and for our ultimate glorification. They were planned with His benediction 'and behold it was very good'. Is this not reassuring? Why, therefore, should not I, frail human that I am, glory in my affliction? It is in love for my soul He ordained every blood test, every X-ray, every radiotherapy treatment and every medication. Cancer is the only ailment by which He could take me along the path He mapped out for me. It is enough that it is my Lord's path for me. Let me not permit the grass of forgetfulness, of indifference, or of neglectfulness grow over it.

'When I think of all the Lord's people I have come in contact with as a consequence of my malady, I feel privileged. When I think of those who visited me, I feel honoured. Lord, let me never underestimate their worth. May it please Thee to beautify my life with the dew of their presence, to love them because they are Thine. Consecrate me Lord, through this illness. At every turn of events, please be there, grant thy protection, grant courage and support me. Help me to witness for Thee, to give Thee the glory, to crucify self - even in illness self is a problem. Praise be to His name He doth promise, 'My grace is sufficient for Thee and my strength is made perfect in weakness'. That wasn't just for Paul or for the church, it is personal to me.

'Lord give me fit preparation for the Eternity to which I must go, perhaps shortly, who knows. Lord be there with me. In the valley, give me the necessary strength and always enable me to act, behave, respond like one of Your children. It is a privilege to be the bearer of cancer in order to witness for Thee'.

Not having read these and the following passages since I returned to work, I would now almost say that the words written therein are not my own. I share them for what they are worth. Unfortunately, the material is not dated. It is given here in the sequence in which it is in my jotter.

Thursday/Raigmore

'Read Psalm 35 at worship this morning. Verse nine was very appropriate:

'And all my bones shall say, O Lord
Who is like unto Thee'.

'Do my bones, the very bones being treated, say this? They have every reason to. Took Philippians Chapter 3 at worship. Read it twice and cannot keep my thoughts under control. Will write as I go along to try and impress the truth on my mind and soul.

'"Finally my brethren, rejoice in the Lord". Verse 1. It doesn't say, rejoice in fair weather, when all is well with my soul. No. I must rejoice in adversity, in affliction, when ill-health is my portion, when the ultimate decline is a reality, but I must also rejoice, in health, in happiness, in friendship and in Him the risen Christ who lives. I think again of His sufferings and the text which says, 'In all their affliction, He was afflicted'. Why, therefore, should I fear the progress of this disease. I need not, He planned it, He will be with me. Oh! how His plan is my strength, I cannot get away from it.

'Help me to pursue the course of life Thou hast mapped out for me by always rejoicing in Thyself, by continuing in the work Thou hast given me to do as if cancer was a nothing or rather, as it is, Thy gift. May I see this episode as an interlude with Thyself. Help me to love my cancer, Lord, to see the necessity of receiving it from Thy gracious hand. Help me to thank Thee for blessings manifold, for upholding grace, for the love Thou hast shown me through caring friends, for the security of Thy promises, for the assurance that Thy grace is and will be sufficient for me.

' "What things were gain to me those I counted loss for Christ" v.7. What a response. O Paul, how committed you were in the service of your Lord. Sadly, I cannot say this. To emphasise his willingness to give all up for Christ Paul goes on, 'Yea doubtless I count all things but loss for the excellency of the knowledge of Christ Jesus my Lord'. Where does this leave me? Far, far short of expectation. Lord, make me what I am not. '..... for whom I have suffered the loss of all things and do count them but dung, that I may win Christ'. Paul, what a wonderful place to be in! This is not achieved through comfortable rest or ease or a 'lack-a-daisical' approach to spiritual things but through crucifying the flesh. You knew what suffering was and it was not the pain of a bone secondary, your spiritual stature grew through inner anguish, the pain of many a varied tempest, of stripes, of imprisonment, of days in the deeps and shipwreck, and yet, you carried on, Paul. Why? Because you counted all things - the joys, the sorrows, the sufferings - but dung that you may win Christ and be found in Him with no righteousness of your own. What could be more demeaning than dung, something fit only to be cast aside, thrown out? O Paul you did have your priorities in the right order. Do I not feel small as I consider this, yes, and very inadequate.

'Verse 10, "That I may know Him and the power of His Resurrection". His resurrection by which we can know the certainty of our own resurrection. What hope this inspires!

'"The fellowship of His Sufferings", same verse. Oh my soul, do you know what this means? I hardly dare to think I do. It means identifying with Himself and it results in understanding, appreciation, a brotherly closeness, a bond of love. I have such a poor understanding of this particular fellowship and I am almost afraid to seek it in case the means by which the Lord might effect it will be too much for me to bear. Is this not selfish? Yes, I do not deserve to enter into the fellowship of His sufferings. Lord, help me!

'"Forgetting those things which are behind and reaching forth to those things which are before ....", verse 13. What grace and what faith! Grace to forget, grace to look forward and faith to advance. 'Reaching forth', that implies vision, a sight of something worth reaching for. It is not inactivity. We cannot reach forth by doing nothing. We have to exercise faith and extend faith so that we may lay hold of those glorious promises which are set before us.

'"I press toward the mark". With urgency we must march onwards and upwards.

'"For our conversation is in Heaven from whence also we look for the Saviour, the Lord Jesus Christ", verse 20. Paul, we have seen how committed you were, how you had your priorities right and now we see how spiritual you are. Not for you the idle conversation that profiteth nothing. But where does this leave me? How do I know my conversation is in Heaven? The text does not say conversation about Heaven. That would be easier. No, it is our conversation in Heaven. What does this imply? Oh!

the shortcomings of my understanding.

'But Paul doesn't stop here, he continues, "who shall change our vile body that it may be fashioned like unto His glorious body....", verse 21. Vile body? Is sin not vile? Has sin not infiltrated every fibre of our being? Paul, you knew what you were talking about, but I would argue that I am much more vile, much more wretched and yet, like you Paul, my vile body will also be fashioned like unto His glorious body. His provision is most wonderful. Vile creatures, such as I, expecting to receive a welcome into His Mansion. When I think of the sins I have committed in the fourteen short years since I first developed cancer I can truly say, "Amazing love that saved a wretch like me". It is this love which fills me with hope that I am numbered among those who will inhabit, in glorious body, the glorious Kingdom, to gaze upon my glorious King and to dwell among a glorious people.'

The next pages in my jotter are taken up with sayings and snippets I read and enjoyed. For example:

'It is God's truth, that one loving spirit can set others on fire ..... More and more I feel that love is the golden secret of life. The very air of Heaven is love, for God is love and love never faileth. So go on loving, not only the loveless but the unlovable, the difficult, the perplexing, the disappointed, unto the end'. (Amy Carmichael)

I thought this was beautiful though I find it difficult to put it into practice.

Saturday/Raigmore

"By my God I have leaped over a wall".

'Interesting that I should be sent this verse today inside a card. It was the verse which spoke to me after my bone scan. Oh! if I could but thank Him for His goodness to me, thank Him for keeping me so well, thank Him for friends upon whose heart He has placed me as a burden, thank

Him for every bouquet of flowers He moved caring friends to send. What a ministry He has prepared for me through His family on earth and, yes, my family. What about the family above? Do they share in what is happening to the family on earth? Surely they do, one Head, one family, whether on earth or in Heaven. What a glorious thought.'

Wednesday/Raigmore

'Spent some time today thinking of those facing Eternity without Christ. How difficult it is to give hope, comfort, inspiration. Sharing Christ in such circumstances can be difficult, yet my heart bleeds for them in their bleak and desolate situation, without God and without hope. He is merciful until the eleventh hour. How could I cope with the seed of mortality in my body if I was bereft of a living faith in a living Saviour? He eases our pains with His Grace and love. Lord, help me to thank Thee, to give Thee all the Glory, all the pre-eminence, to be eternally grateful for the path Thou has taken me. Help me to witness and not be ashamed to own thy cause and O Lord, destroy the pride in my heart. Even as I write, it rears its ugly head. Thou art my only hope in time and for Eternity'.

> *'I'd rather gather roses without thorns, Lord,*
> *A bright and fragrant, beautiful bouquet*
> *To decorate my world with pretty pleasures,*
> *The brambles and the briars I'll throw away*
> *But you say that I must pluck the thorns as well, Lord,*
> *Though they'll pierce my heart and sting my soul*
> *You say that pain is part of peace,*
> *You tell me that breaking is a part of being whole.'*

chapter eighteen

Weep Not

'I lived to die and now I die to live and do enjoy more than I did believe'.

When the Mayflower sailed out of Plymouth in 1620 the Pilgrims had little concept of the dangers the voyage held, particularly during the winter when blizzards blinded their vision and ice froze the cordage which supported the masts and distended their sails. On one such occasion the pilot or helmsman called out, "Be of good cheer, I see the harbour", only minutes later to cry, "Lord be merciful to us, my eyes never saw this place before". Overcome by fear and nervousness he would have made shipwreck but for the efforts of his fellow mariners. Thus they found themselves quite soon in the lee of an island. A certain writer, reflecting on this experience, says, "Though they had been a day and a night in much trouble and danger, God gave them a morning of comfort and refreshing".

Does not this account typify the pilgrimage of the Christian, who, setting out on the life of faith is unaware of what the journey may hold? Many Christians, on their first spiritual high, have concluded that the journey was to be one of sunshine all the way, only to discover that lows follow highs, as night follows day. The blizzards of trouble and the icy cold of indifference often perplexes the heart, and causes the Christian to cry out, 'Lord be merciful to me, my eyes have never seen this place before'. They become fearful that they may make spiritual shipwreck before they reach their safe haven. One minute they view the harbour of God's love and head there, the next they are bewildered by experiences unknown to them. Like the Children of Israel they wander through the wilderness, learning that their Elims' are preceded by their Marahs', that their peace is interrupted by spiritual conflict and their best intentions overcome by sinful weaknesses. Distressed, they cry unto the Lord, conscious that He is their only refuge. It is of this people Moses said, 'Happy art thou O, Israel: who is like unto thee, a people saved by the Lord'. Yes, this is the Christian's walk, a pilgrimage, whether like Iain, of whom this chapter speaks, the journey is cut short in youth or, as in my own case, prolonged into middle or perhaps even old age. Of this pilgrimage, Sir Walter Raleigh, with such insight, wrote:

'Give me my scallop - shell of quiet,
My staff of faith to walk upon,
My scrip of joy, immortal diet,
My bottle of salvation,
My gown of glory, hope's true gage;
And thus I'll take my pilgrimage'.

During the three episodes of my own cancer I felt as though I was sheltering in the harbour of His love, but I couldn't remain there. Refreshed, I must move on, for there was a race to be won. As my pilgrimage took me once more outwith the hospital doors and towards home, I marvelled at how God had prospered me. My treatment concluded on a Friday morning; I travelled home in the afternoon and I was back at work the following Tuesday. I was absent from work for only two weeks, no longer than a normal holiday absence.

On my return to the Island I encountered two persons who told me they had dreamt of me. Continuing my jottings at the time, I recorded those. One person saw me walk towards an attractive house but she could not keep up with me. She was unaware at the time that I was in hospital and when she heard, concluded that this was the interpretation of the dream. The other person recounted seeing me in the old family home, long since vacated. We were singing from the Song of

Solomon, 'I am the Rose of Sharon and the Lily of the Valley', What was common to both persons was their reluctance to share their dreams with me in case the telling would disturb me. As a consequence the following flowed into my thoughts and emerged from my pen:

' "Jehovah hear thee in the day when trouble He doth send". He will, He has done. My peace cometh from this Great Jehovah, a peace born out of His love for me. Nothing can alter that, though He may for a season remove His presence in order to teach me the need of dependence upon Himself and not on the peace I may be experiencing.

'My thoughts are drawn to the loveliest of Lilies. Imagine descending into the Valley to be met and accompanied by this Lily. Oh! the sheer loveliness of Christ, the Christian's Lily. What holiness, what beauty, what purity, what serenity, what fragrant companionship, what eternity in the One who is the journeying friend in the Valley. May my whole heart be captivated as He accompanies me, so that I may grow more and more like Him. Let His loveliness draw me until in admiration I look steadily upon Him; let His Holiness fill me with desire until I seek to be holy as He is Holy; let His Purity lead me to behold my corruption and loath my sin; let His Serenity calm my spirit and fill my soul with peace; let His Beauty, born out of His Sufferings and marked with the scars of the Cross, transfix my gaze until in wonder I cry out, 'My Lord and my God'. Oh! may His excellencies mould my thoughts and actions until they are at one with His will and my heart and flesh cry out for the living God.

'How different the reality from the desire. When the pruning knife or the quiet teaching of His love is removed how quickly I succumb to my unruly nature. My desires become worldly, my affections cold, my manner aloof, my prayers vain and empty, my meditation careless, my diligence to His Word dilatory, my works fit only to be burnt and my love lukewarm. Oh! that lukewarmness! Little wonder the Lord wished to spew the Church of the Laodiceans out of His mouth - Lord guard me against the dominance of my old nature and bring my will under the subjection of Thy Holy Command. Enable me to breathe in the perfume of the Rose of Sharon and the Lily of the Valley so that I may exude their fragrance and their essence to Thy Glory. Let pride not have precedence but let my life be consecrated to thy service. Give grace to stand the test otherwise I will fail utterly.'

During the Spring Communion season, about a month before I went back into hospital, a group of young people gathered in my home on Friday evening. Among them a quiet, gentle lad of nineteen years who had been converted a year previously and who professed faith six months later. It was the first time we had met and he willingly shared with us his testimony. There was an aura of saintliness about him which was difficult to comprehend and I felt an urge to encourage him, which I did after worship. I never forgot him. Six weeks later when I returned from sick leave I learned Iain was very unwell. His diagnosis - cancer.

At that time his parents and family were unknown to me but the profound effect his illness produced in everyone I met compelled me to write my own immediate response.

At Home.
5th May 1992

'Heard today of Iain's illness. Everyone is so saddened by it. He was here on Friday night of our last communion. A quiet unassuming Christian, young in life and young in grace, he touched me so deeply that I felt urged to speak with him and try to encourage him.

'I cannot be sad. Am I abnormal or is it just that I have cancer myself? I hope it is not ignorance. But much as I would wish my reactions to be different I can only be as I am. Those who spoke with me spoke with great sadness and seemed askance at my apparent unfeeling reaction, as if I were rebuking them. This is not so. I am as I am and I cannot force my thoughts and feelings into any other mould.

'Few may be Iain's years, but age means nothing to the Lord. Whether nineteen or eighty nine it makes no difference to Him. He works out His own purposes. We creatures of time are so governed by age that we cannot calculate aright. We tend to think that usefulness in the life of grace comes with advancing years and when youth is cut down our thoughts turn to the Cause. But the instrument and the Cause are His. The Reaper has a right to reap as and when He pleases. I can only think, how fortunate Iain is to have been called from darkness to light in his youth and then, possibly, to be called Home while still of tender age and heart, yes, called Home before the ravages of a sinful nature influence his thoughts and actions. Pause, my soul, and think of the sins from which he will be kept, as a consequence of being ripened almost as soon as he flourished. When I compare this with my own life. alas, 'All is vanity'.

'If Iain did not know the Lord, how very tragic and sad his circumstances would be, but he does, and the Lord will uphold him, I pray he will receive the tidings of his illness with Christian fortitude and a clarity that the Lord's Will is right - May the Lord be very close to you Iain, very very special, a real present aid in your time of need and because He cannot deny Himself, He will. His promises are sure and steadfast, 'His mercies are new every morning, Great is His faithfulness'.

'It is the duty of the Church to pray for Iain and for all those entering into the Valley - I am sure, Iain, you will be conscious of their prayers and it will be their privilege to remember you. May you be surrounded as with a wall of fire for there is no time Satan is more active than when he recognises a soul is almost out of his reach. He targets that soul hoping somehow to win it for himself. His desire is to prevent the soul from entering the Celestial City; as if he could! But his fiery darts wound and these wounds can cause the soul much anguish. Let us be alive to the fact that Satan knows when his opportunity is short and he often presents himself under a very different guise. He is then much more cunning and deceitful in his endeavour to trouble the soul. Any thought which will make the Christian forget his Lord, make him err in his judgement regarding the Lord's dealings and draw him away from the source of his comfort, is his delight. Satan never gives up until the soul is beyond his reach. I wish we considered this more often and called to mind fellow believers, as they approach the Jordan, with vehement conviction in our prayers on their behalf - Lord, place the Children of the Valley as a burden on our hearts until remembering them at Thy Throne becomes as natural as breathing. O! soul of the believer, descending into the Valley, your Lord is there with you; your family will be there too, albeit on the fringe, watching, waiting, observing, ready to comfort, to love and support. Your brothers and sisters in Christ, whose union will not be broken at death as natural ties will, are honoured to witness the flight of your soul to its Maker and to help carry you, by their prayers, over the Jordan. What honour Christ has placed on weak earthern vessels. When my turn comes, be there, Lord, and may thy Children be there too.

The Lord will not lose one soul for whom He has died. This is most reassuring, but it does not mean that we may not experience fear when we see death on the horizon. Christian, in John Bunyan's Pilgrim's Progress, found that his feet could not reach the bottom as he entered into the River Jordan of death and he was afraid that he would sink. But this was not for long. We too may have fearsome thoughts. We may fear we will sink in the Jordan as the streams of our thoughts almost carry us away. We may fear we will lose awareness of His abiding presence and feel as though we have moved out of the orbit of His everlasting arms. We will fear when our sense of sufficiency in Him is lost and billow after billow breaks over our soul as Satan's assaults continue to flow fast and furious. But as with Christian day break is at hand and the shore on the Heavenward side of the river is in sight - keep going my soul, keep your eyes fastened on the King in His beauty and the land which is closer than when you first believed. By faith grasp the promises, by hope see the unseen, by love clasp Him to your bosom and feel His reciprocal response as you hear Him whisper, 'Until the day break and the shadows flee away, turn my beloved....' and you surprise yourself as you say, 'My beloved is mine and I am His'.

'O! sweet whispers of Eternal love; who can know it, who can understand it? 'My Grace is sufficient for thee' - Iain, may you know this to be true as you pass through the waters and through the rivers, which will not overflow you and as you walk through the fire, may you realise it cannot burn you nor its flame as much as kindle upon you. Why? Because 'I am the Lord your God' - May this, O Lord, be my portion also when my time comes. May I be found precious in your sight, precious because Thy Dear Son died on the Cross of Calvary for me. How I wish I could see more deeply into this wonderful transaction. I feel as though something evades my understanding. I wish I had more feeling about it but by faith I must grasp it or I sink.

'How can I think of myself as honourable in His sight, as precious in His eyes, as loved and beloved. 'Men given for me and people for my life'. Whatever that may mean. But these are promises which are true of His Children and I confess to a gracious and lively hope that I am numbered among them. As one of old said, "All the 'fear nots, for I am with you' are mine", why should I not therefore bask in their comfort. I do, but alas! for so short a time. Endless are the thoughts, words and deeds with which I break His Commandments and this causes much spiritual discomfort. "He that loveth me keepeth my commandments". Was ever a Christian such a conundrum? Yet, I stand four square on the finished work of Calvary. Nothing more, nothing less will qualify me or you, Iain, for an audience with the King of Glory.

'Iain, however clouded your vision of Him at this moment, He is there with you; He is in your heart, in your life, at your bedside, in your family, in your visitors and best of all in His promises. He is unseen and yet seen. He is a Saviour who Himself went through the process of death, without sin and without seeing corruption in His flesh, to rise triumphant, and so will you and so will I. Surely this enables us to say, 'O! death, where is they sting? O! grave where is thy victory?' The sting is removed, like a snake deprived of its venom it is rendered harmless. When Death, the last enemy, is conquered, the graves will no longer hold our precious dust, precious because still united to Christ. On the resurrection morn when the archangel will sound the trumpet, and the graves give up their sleeping dead, you will rise Iain, triumphant, and with you will be the many who at this moment, mourn over you. To die is indeed gain.'

> *'I would not change my blest estate*
> *For all the world calls good or great*
> *And whilst my faith can keep her hold*
> *I envy not the sinners gold'.*

I visited Iain twice during his stay in hospital. I found him bright and resigned to his condition. He was to commence chemotherapy but I was a little uncertain as to his understanding of this. He was but nineteen years old and it must not be expected that he could grasp all that was happening to him. His conversation was of spiritual things and it was lovely, in the midst of his sufferings, to see him so wonderfully in harmony with his circumstances.

I had never met Iain's parents until he became a patient in the Hospice, eleven weeks after his operation. I felt an immediate affinity with them, a bond through their son. 'And a three fold cord is not quickly broken'. Who can understand this, the invisible fellowship between Christ, Iain, his family and myself. What began in Eternity, manifested in my home, through Iain's visit, four months previously. Spurgeon used to say, that the saints militant are of the same host as the saints triumphant, that those who are suffering are of the same company as the glorified, the sick son of the same family as his brother in perfect health. Some, their griefs coming to an end, knowing no tears, but others having to wait awhile to battle, wrestle and to suffer. Those already arrived and those on the way are described as one company.

Iain was with us but for five brief days when the Lord gathered His young and tender bud. In his brief life Iain made a great impression on those around him. His popularity was evident by the numbers of young and old who called to see him. One person was particularly dear to him and learning of this I contacted him. He came and they spent about an hour together. We never knew what they conversed about, but it was obvious that Iain was greatly strengthened as a consequence.

How willingly He can make His children part with what He has loaned to them. 'The Lord gave and the Lord taketh away', is the expression of a heart in agreement with what God is requiring. This was evident in this family. Observing them, I thought of the woman of Naan to whom Christ so tenderly said, "weep not". "He was not", as I once read, "forbidding the expression of emotion, no, He had Himself wept, but He was tenderly and with compassion taking stricken hearts unto Himself".

When the missionary, Jack Harrison, lay dying at the age of forty five his words were, "Hallelujah, I am ready. I thought my work was not yet done but if God sees otherwise, His is the last word. No miserable passing out for me, no defeat, only triumph". The testimony of William Hewling, a prisoner in the interests of religious freedom in England, is similar. When he was condemned to die he was nineteen years of age, the same age as Iain. Many wished he could be spared execution but what had he to say? "I would not stay behind for ten thousand worlds". He then knelt and prayed for his enemies and for the presence of God to support his friends. Rising from his knees he said, "My joy and comfort now is that I have a Christ to go to", and with a smile on his countenance he submitted himself to the scaffold.

Are these accounts, separated as they are from Iains', by some three hundred years, so very different from his? No. Iain had his suffering, he had his youth, he had his triumph and I am sure he thought his work for his Lord was not yet done. If he could have conversed at the end, I think the words of William Hewling would have expressed his feelings, 'I would not stay behind for ten thousand worlds ....It is my joy and comfort now that I have a Christ to go to'. This is the expression and comfort of every departing believer.

On the last evening of Iain's life on earth I called in to see him, as was my practice, before going home. His mother was sitting quietly by his bedside, watching her son while he slept. After a brief conversation with her, I moved from the bedside towards the door. His mother then called out that Iain was beckoning me. I returned and taking a hold of his outstretched hand said a few words to him. I felt these were so inadequate that, on impulse, I bent down and kissed him. I knew it was our farewell, even if he were spared until the morning, which in fact he was. I recount this because of the loveliness I personally saw and felt at the death bed of this gentle lamb of Christ's flock. Though his sufferings were great he was never heard to complain. "I'm more in love with the Lord Jesus Christ every day", he said to a friend who enquired as to how he was. With complete resignation he gave himself over to the Will of his Master, 'O! Lamb of God I come'. He was led victorious through his short Christian life, to die triumphant in Him, a trophy of His Grace.

'I lived to die, now I die that I might live and enjoy more than I believed.'

chapter nineteen

Cancer ~ Day By Day

'Behind my life the weaver stands and works his wondrous will'.

"**D**o you know anything about Satan?", I asked the visiting Specialist sitting opposite me. Nonplussed, he answered, "To try and keep out of his way!". He was discussing with me the fact that I had been X-rayed since he last saw me at his clinic. My divergence from the main thrust of his questioning must have been perplexing, but I knew it would become clear to him and so I continued by enquiring as to his knowledge of the text, 'But Satan hindered us'. Without waiting for a response I explained how Paul would have gone to the Thessalonians, but Satan hindered him.

A week before I was due to go to Switzerland on holiday I developed a pain which left me limping for a day or two. It was sudden in onset and I couldn't account for it. Anxious friends enquired as to the wisdom of proceeding with my plans. Finally, I agreed that if the pain persisted into the middle of the week I would see about it. After all, I was due to leave for Switzerland on the Saturday. Wednesday came, the pain was still there and so I contacted my doctor. The outcome was a consultation followed by X-rays. It was then that the words '.... Satan hindered ....' arrested my thoughts. Could he be trying to prevent me from going to Switzerland? I believed he was. By the time I saw the Consultant on the Friday the pain had gone.

What is it like to live day by day with the knowledge of cancer? I speak personally and only of breast cancer. I do not find it any different from the period when I lived without it. True, there are external attitudes to which I am now subjected, but the internal responses may be experienced by anyone in any health situation, while the feelings of failure in the struggle with a deceitful heart and the machinations of Satan are but a part of the Christian's warfare and not an outcome of the disease.

For the majority of people suffering from cancer, there is always a reminder in the series of clinical consultations to which they are subjected and the medication required to be taken day by day. This is likely to continue from diagnosis through remission and into the terminal phase of the disease, should this indeed be the outcome. But this isn't the only reminder. The Chapter begins with a dialogue consequential upon a diagnostic X-ray, a common practice once cancer is confirmed and yet another reminder of the disease. The concern of friends, obvious in the opening paragraph, is actually very real. Complain of something, admit to excessive tiredness or just appear below par and one of two scenarios present. If the complaint appears mild, apprehension will be expressed. Through auto-suggestion, this may eventually influence the persons concerned until their thoughts carry them to the point of consideration. "Maybe there is something there .... perhaps I should be sensible and look into it ....". Forgotten by all is the fact that cancer does not mean exemption from other ailments. It seems as if any disorder can only be a further episode of this malady. It is wise to exclude the simple before jumping to conclusions, but how many do? If I suffered from skeletal problems before my cancer, should I not now be just as liable as anyone else to recurrent episodes? Of course I should. Cancer is no guarantee against this.

The second scene is in the reverse. Pain may be more severe, symptoms more defined, warning bells ringing, yet friends and acquaintances hasten to quieten our fears, often suggesting something quite elementary. "Of course it is nothing serious", they assure us, "It couldn't possibly be: it is probably muscular". Has anything really changed? Listen to the insights of Florence Nightingale, 'There is scarcely a greater worry which the sick have to endure then the incurable hopes of their friends ..., attempting to cheer the sick by making light of their danger and exaggerating their possibilities of recovery ... The fact is the patient is not cheered at all by these well meaning but tiresome friends, on the contrary they are depressed and wearied'. How true this runs to experience. If, in these circumstances, well-meaning friends acknowledged the problem, awaited the outcome and ceased to offer platitudes, they would energise rather than enervate. Listening is untold service.

The other 'little foxes' which spoil the vines of daily living are, though diminutive, nonetheless tiresome. Take, for instance, the common form of address. On meeting someone it is usual to say, 'Good Morning', or some similar greeting. If the person addressed has been unwell, this greeting may be followed with, 'How are you keeping?', or 'Are you feeling better?'. If the response is in the affirmative the question is unlikely to be asked again. Observe what happens when the person concerned has had cancer. The greeting, 'How are you keeping ...... are you well?' continues to be asked again and again. A slight inflection on the words is clearly discernible.

Then there is the question, and I have been asked this many times over the last fourteen years, which was addressed to me recently by the practice nurse when I collected my prescription. "Are you still working?" Lay persons may be forgiven for thinking thus but professionals ...?, Well, perhaps I have by now come to expect it of all groups. My own thinking was not dissimilar at one time. "Why", I asked this particular nurse, "is it thought I should not still be working?". There was no response.

A friend who is a health visitor and whom I have not seen for some time, recently contacted me by telephone. After the usual opening remarks the conversation went something like this, " .... and how are you really keeping .... you're quite amazing .... I mean it is a long time since your illness first began and you have had those recurrences .... surely this is unusual .... do you think you are in remission?" Are those thoughts so very strange? Not at all. There are very many people who think thus about cancer. They may never venture to express their astonishment quite so directly to the person concerned, but they will to their friends. Longevity and cancer are not compatible in the minds of the majority, or even in the minds of many Christians.

Influenced by the same sentiment, emotion rather than reason, are those who continually tell you that you are looking well. The expectation, of course, is that this should encourage or inspire hope in the person spoken with. Instead, it often creates an awareness that the condition is being continually assessed. The prospect that the cancer person should not look or feel well, or have the energy to do a particular job is by public opinion, standard. 'Well cancer', does not rest comfortably with the majority. Had I presented with some other illness, reactionary concern would long since have ceased.

Another 'little fox' is the awkwardness that ensues when having spent some time in the company of a group unaware of your circumstances, someone suddenly divulges your medical history. There is an immediate and perceptible change of interest in you and you quickly become aware of it. Confidences and insecurities are now shared. Friends and relatives having the disease and even those who may have died from it, are discussed freely. The reaction of some in the group may, of course, be very different. A few tend to avoid you in their effort to protect themselves. They don't know how to handle this knowledge; they are embarrassed, and it frightens them. Others may be so touched by the fact that you have to live with cancer that they treat you with veneration.

Responses are very similar when called upon to address an audience, large or small. Whenever your condition is known, attention is rapt. Following the conclusion of the session, people want to speak with you, frequently making respectful comments about your condition. They seem drawn .... almost in wonder .... to the normality of it all. Reactions like these suggest that cancer is still viewed differently from other diseases. Why? It has to be fear.

I recently read in one of the newspapers an article which reflects the antiquated views which are still held in some circles. The writer was suggesting that the name cancer should be dropped from cervical cancer tests. She said the name cancer frightens women and could, therefore, put them off having this test. I find it extremely perplexing, in our so called enlightened society, that such retrograde thinking should persist. This lady wanted another name to be found for cervical cytology which would reflect it as a preventive measure, which in fact it is. Thankfully, it is the opinion of one woman although it is probably reflective of the fears and concerns of many of her generation. But where do we stand as Christians? Could we not bring a more positive attitude to bear upon this disease?

Twenty five thousand women are diagnosed with breast cancer each year, in the United Kingdom. The problem is not going to go away, not in the near future at least, yet, statistics show that survival rate is on the increase and while it remains an unpredictable cancer, large numbers diagnosed die of totally unrelated diseases, while others live many useful years before their illness reaches the terminal phase. All this was known to the professional who wrote, "When a close relative found a lump in her breast I had buried her in my mind before discovering it was benign". If persons engaged in cancer related work can write so honestly of their reactions, is it any wonder that those out in the big world respond as they do?

These are all attitudinal or external issues which spring from reactionary responses that have not seriously diminished over the years. But what about the internal working out of subjective thought, that which governs the mind of persons with cancer, about their cancer? This is extremely difficult to quantify. Thought process occasioned by this disease, is not something people share very easily and it can differ widely from person to person. A study on the subject could throw up interesting results. However, I venture to suggest that our thoughts, feelings and concerns are not so very different from those familiar to the rest of humanity, whatever their affliction. For instance, I might question, 'Is this pain or that symptom related to my cancer, is this state of tiredness due to overwork, stress or age, or is it symptomatic of something serious? Should I raise these matters with my doctor or wait until my next clinic appointment? Am I being neurotic and wasting my doctor's time? Will my doctor think so?' The Christian is not superhuman and should not try to be so. Why should we have anxious thoughts about sharing our concerns? God made provision for us through the skills with which he endowed the medical profession. Relieving concerns is as important as relieving any pressing symptom and all human beings experience these at some time. It has been suggested that cancer undermines the person's confidence and therefore there is a greater level of concern than normal. This may be so generally, but I have certainly not been aware of it personally.

Mind-travel is not exclusively taken up with aches and pains and such like concerns. There are other halting places for the 'mind-troops', simple matters which may present a dilemma for the cancer person. "Yes, I am marginally overweight. Do I leave off the niceties and get my weight down? Is that tempting providence?". Being a realist I expect a day to come when I may not have an appetite for food, should I not, therefore, continue to enjoy the little luxuries while I can? Another quandary may relate to retirement, "Should I continue to work for as long as my health permits or retire and appreciate what may be left of my healthy life?" These are paltry examples but they reflect the disquiet and uncertainties which may perplex someone with cancer. Reproach should not be cast on the thinker, particularly if the person is an unbeliever. The Christian has a resource centre to which he or she goes with all unfounded or unsubstantive thought. Here they draw on the guiding wisdom of Eternal Love, deriving therefrom regulating principles for thoughts and actions.

Consider now the thoughts of those without cancer. They are equally introspect, perhaps more so. "I wonder if this perpetual headache is associated with my raised blood pressure. Should I have it checked or will I leave it meantime? That pain in my calf, is it muscular? It can't be my varicose veins, its too painful, I hope it isn't a clot? Perhaps I should make an appointment with my doctor. I'll leave it for a day or two until I see if it goes away. Palpitations again! I was out of breath walking up that incline. Stress or anxiety, it can't be this time? Could it be from my heart? Why ever did I agree to that hip replacement; what if I don't survive the anaesthetic?". These are all fairly typical of the health related anxieties of our population. The point at issue is that concern about health or ill health is not the prerogative of the cancer person. Every human being at some time experiences unease which imposes upon the faculty of their reasoning. In this we are all alike and living with the knowledge of cancer does not alter it or add to it.

Moving on to the weightier matters of living with a potentially serious disease. I must have been pretty naive in my thinking for I had imagined that in such circumstances I would spend what was left of my life making sure of my calling and my election. I thought I would live a life of holy application to all that God commanded, remaining in close fellowship with Him as I lived out His Will. My activities would be given to prayer, reading the word, communion with Him, commitment and consecration. Looking back over the years since my cancer was discovered I can but say, 'It is of the Lord's mercies that I have not been consumed'. I wish I could say that during this time I lived hour by hour and day by day in harmony with His Will, a heart surrendered, knowing the joy of obedience. Instead I have known moments when I could have wished that the Lord had taken me Home at the time of diagnosis. What a heap of sins I would have been prevented from committing!

It is wrong, however, to assume that there weren't moments of joy unspeakable in the presence of my Lord, moments for which I am thankful I was left on earth to experience them. But despite this, my many sins, the corruption of my nature and the imperfections of my spiritual life have caused me on numerous occasions to pace the floor as with sighs and tears I brought my failings before Him. Contrast this with the ideals I expected of myself, and of any Christian whose illness is of an uncertain nature, and it will be understood why I have longed for perfection and why there have been moments when I longed to be able to escape from myself. Yet, through all the discouragements of temptation and the consequences of sin, my companion, the grace called Hope never left me, hope based upon His faithfulness, faithfulness to the promises of His Word. Yes, in repentance I turned to the Lord for forgiveness and I do so again and again as I continue to fail. Oh! how long-suffering His love to such a wayward believer. 'Thy love to me was wonderful'.

'Drink of His flagons then, thou Church, thou dove,
And eat His apples, who art sick of love'.

Moody Stuart, speaking on the remembrance of sin in Heaven, has this to say, "When God remembers our sin no more, He does not cease to know that we have sinned, but in His own mercy, through the blood of the Lamb, He loves and delights in the redeemed as much as if they had never sinned and much more. We will love much because we are forgiven much. We would regret not to remember, because we shall so rejoice and so glorify Christ in washing us whiter than snow. Adam can never forget his sin, but the remembrance of it in heaven does not lessen his everlasting peace". My sins are so awful that my immediate reaction was, "Oh! no, I don't want ever to remember them", but if I accept that their remembrance will add to my thankfulness and everlasting joy, as I thank God for cleansing me, then the argument put forward by Moody Stuart is quite exhilarating.

Before leaving the subject of living with cancer the question must be asked; what have I learned as a consequence of living with it from day to day? Have I, as a result, gone about my Father's business with renewed fervour? Has it earned anything for my Lord? I am account-able to Him for the use to which I put all the gifts He gifteth to me; have I used this one to His Glory?

When I read the account of Cripple Tom; a poor, sick, destitute, cripple, I felt so ashamed of my own witness. He used to say, "Knowin' is lovin', lovin' is doin'. It ain't love without". He did all he could for his Master. He used to write texts and drop them from his attic window in the hope that someone would be blessed. Once when praying, he was heard to say, "I know You're a listenin'. This friend is having a bit of trouble about not havin' worked enough for Thee. Will You help him to see to it that there's nothin' left undone in comin' days". Tom's love, his obedience, his work and his desire for the furtherance of the Cause, fills me with shame as I review my mis-spent time and energies. And yet, I must admit to a desire, that the gift of cancer entrusted to me might not be solely for myself, but by His Grace, a help and an encouragement to others.

I have prayed that I would love my cancer because He planned it for me, and I can say, in all honesty, I see it as a messenger of His love to my soul, an earnest, a pledge, a token for good, and I dearly long to use it in His service. As a stone thrown into the water creates ever widening circles, so by His spirit I would like Him to use this cancer to create waves of blessings which would reach someone's heart.

Has my cancer made me a better or a wiser person, a better or a wiser Christian? Sadly not. I continue to wax and wane, to rise and fall, the same as ever I did, and when I consider my impious thoughts and ponder my impious ways, I feel quite discouraged by my performance as a Christian. My heart swerves and falters; where is the distinctive mark of the Christian? Am I a poor example? Yes, but I would be poorer still without the love-gift of malignant disease. I count it a privilege to bear it. Through it, I have been taught my own littleness before Him, and I have seen His mightiness, His long-suffering and His infinite power.

How very wonderful that a time will yet come, a happy time, a time of majestic splendour, when cleansed from all the impurities of sin, the Believer will see the King in His beauty. Satan's whispers shut out forever. Corrie Ten Boom used so expressively to say, ".... the devil is a good cattle dealer who walks round a cow once and knows all her weak spots!" He has certainly known mine and putting his knowledge to good use has often discouraged me.

May I, and the readers of this book, bring our sicknesses and our health to the feet of Him who gifts all. Remember our health is closer because Heaven is nearer. There is balm in Gilead, there is a Physician there. With His balm and the touch of His hand He heals our every ailment, while, as sweet smelling myrrh, He pours His love into our hearts until our senses appreciate His beauty and the joy of the Lord becomes our strength.

> *'Could we with ink the ocean fill,*
> *And were the skies with parchment made,*
> *Was every stalk on earth a quill*
> *And every man a scribe to trade.*
> *To write the love of God above,*
> *Would drain the ocean dry.*
> *Nor could the scroll contain the whole,*
> *Though stretched from sky to sky'.*

chapter twenty

God's Chariot

'Come, for all things are now ready'.

It is said of Prince Albert, the Prince Consort, that death found him looking to the Saviour of sinners for dying grace. One of his physicians said to him, "Your Royal Highness will be better in a few days", to which he replied, "No, I shall not recover. I am not taken by surprise, I am not afraid. I trust I am prepared". Baptist Noel writes, "These words from the lips of a man who knew the claims of God and the way of salvation, express hope. The Prince knew that Jesus is the propitiation for our sins, that it is only when we are justified by faith that we have peace with God".

Why have I chosen to begin this last chapter with this testimony? Simply because it is a beautiful end to a full and privileged life. Here is a man of royal blood, rich in worldly possessions and advantaged above many. Yet, we observe in his dying declaration; trust, hope, peace, confidence and serenity. Characteristics which elude many. Irrespective of rank we die poor unless we know the love of Christ which passeth knowledge and are filled with the fullness of God. I think it was Lady Huntingdon who expressed gratitude on reading the words '.... not many noble....', by saying, "Thanks be to God, He hasn't written, 'not any noble'".

This book represents a journey through life and it is, therefore, most natural that it should conclude with the final episode of living - dying and death. On this weighty of events, the receding of the ocean of life, my thoughts must linger. As they do I am aware of my need of real discernment in approaching so lofty a subject. May He, who alone gives unmerited grace, give the necessary inspiration, so that our meditation of the Valley is most sweet.

When I ponder what is left of my own life it concerns me that I will go on as in the past, one minute full of zeal and commitment to my Lord's cause, the next, on account of my sins, in the miry clay of David's fearful pit, mourning my failures and seeking repentance. When I am quickened to the fact that God sees me, not as I see myself but in the spotless robe of His righteousness, I am overwhelmed by God's provision in Christ, by the steadfastness of His electing love - 'a settled principle', as Spurgeon calls it - and by the immutability of His Grace. 'Consolation will never be found in feelings but in the Atonement'. All my sins washed away forever! Every single one of them! Truly 'He raiseth the poor from the dust and lifteth the needy out of the dung hill that He may set him with the princes of His people'.

This book is entitled 'To Everything a Purpose' and there is no greater purpose to life than death, no greater victory than through faith in our Lord Jesus Christ. We know the purpose for which we have been created and the purpose of God's afflicting hand. We know the blessedness of health and we know the blessedness of sickness, but we know little of the blessedness which may yet be ours in the process of dying. We know the purpose in the death of Christ and we know that as a consequence of it, a blessed state awaits the soul of the believer on the other side of the Jordan of death. Evans, referring to the death of Christ has this to say, 'He gave Himself - His whole self .... the whole of His person as God-Man, all that was in man to suffer and all that was in God to merit. He gave His whole life, He gave us His death and this He gave freely'. When I first read these few lines the words which came into my mind were, '.... bound in the bundle of life with the Lord thy God'.

'My name from the palms of His Hands
Eternity will not erase
Impressed on His heart it remains
In marks of indelible grace
Yes, I to the end will endure
As sure as the earnest is given
More happy but not more secure
The glorified spirits in heaven.'

We have lived all our days expecting to die, yet, how often have we really thought about it? Perhaps as a consequence of the seed of disease in my body, I am given to dwell upon it more frequently. By God's grace I do not find it a morbid subject, but one which is a solemn reminder of my accountability to God. But what does take place when death draws nigh, when the struggles of life are almost over and our eternal destiny is about to be settled forever? The truth is we do not know. We may have observed loved ones, friends and others during their confrontation with the last enemy without ever understanding the reality of their circumstances. We know that God's saints bear the image of the heavenly and will be like Him in purity and in happiness in their glorified bodies; we know that the covenant of God is our security; we know that the power of faith strengthens us when we come to die but we do not know the feelings, perceptions or the sensations produced in these moments of final dissolution. Not one of those whom Jesus raised from the dead made reference to the dissolution of their bodies or to what this process could be likened. Scripture remains silent on the transition between life and death, that period of time during which mental and physical changes take place which is known to us as dying. Should we, mere mortals, presume to venture an opinion on the state of sinking into death when we know this is but to enter into things unknown?

Speaking on this topic, Spurgeon writes, 'The Holy Ghost has given us few death bed scenes because being present with us He presents them to us frequently in actual flesh and blood, visible to our eyes, audible to our ears. We are to look upon the presence of the Holy Spirit in the witness of dying men as in some sense in continuance of the Holy

Spirit's instructive authorship. He is writing fresh stanzas to the Glory of God in the deaths of departing saints'. Before we stand, metaphorically speaking, by the bedsides of some of these departed saints, to learn from their experience something of the solitary sojourn into the Valley of Death, let us listen to what F.W. Robertson has to say on dying:

'Brethren, faith tells us one thing our sensations another. There is a world of untold sensations crowded into a moment when a man feels the damp upon his forehead which tells him his hour has come. Sensation in its fullness can come but once.... It is mockery for a man to speak lightly of that which he cannot fully know till it comes.... Our life is connected with a shape, a form, a body of materialism; and now it is palpably melting away into nothingness. The boldest heart may be excused a shudder when there is forced upon it the idea of ceasing forever. It is with the intense passion of being that the idea of death clashes. Search why we shrink from it and we find it presents to us the idea of not being.... We may conquer doubt and fear when we are dying but that is not conquering death....'. While Robertson is quite right in what he says, his logic leaves me unaffected. It fails to excite the emotions or stir up the heart with happy longings for the time when the shades of the evening sun sink below the horizon of life and the dawn of Heaven breaks in the sweet summer morn of Immanuel's land.

Not every Christian is aware of the dawn chorus of the heavenly morn, not every Christian has doubtless assurance. Boswell has this to say of Dr. Johnson, 'He owned that our being in an unhappy uncertainty as to our salvation was mysterious and said, "We must await deliverance in another state of being to have many things explained to us"'. Suggesting to him that Dr. Dodd seemed willing to die, he responded, "Dr. Dodd would have given both his hands and both his legs to have lived. The better a man is the more afraid he is of death, having a clearer view of infinite purity".

The thought of being afraid to die because of the view of infinite purity is most striking. It is one I never came across before, certainly not in the account of any of the death bed scenes I researched while writing this chapter. I include it for this very reason.

Speculating on my own death bed, I wonder if I will be in darkness of soul and intellect or in the clear light of assurance. Will sin weigh heavily, obscuring my view of Him and causing me in my low estate to cry for mercy. 'It is beautiful', writes one, 'to see the repentance of a dying saint'. Will this be my portion? Sometimes, when I ponder thus, I have a calm confidence as I think of the separating of my soul and body, an inner assurance that 'His spirit witnesseth with my spirit', that I am one of His children. But there are other times when I find myself afraid of this unfamiliar and lonesome event. I may not have relatives from whom parting will be painful, but I am still comfortable with the known, this world where I have tabernacled all the days of my life. If I permit my thoughts to dwell here for long I find I have a strange reluctance to die and so I quickly turn my eye heavenward to Christ, 'the deep, sweet, well of love', and call to mind that to depart and be with Him is far better. Dwelling on the Ocean of the fullness of His love produces a warm glow of happiness which weans me to the other side. Who can then but long for the glories which are to follow. 'Oh! how distinguishing is that love!', writes Evans, 'The love of the best of God's Saints has its ebbs and flows .... but here there is no ebb and flow, full tide ever, spring tide at its highest always. He loves His people out of darkness into light. He loves them into love, loves them into Heaven, loves them into God's presence and will there fill them with His love to all eternity'. What comfort! Who wouldn't want to die to enjoy love consummate?

If I had my desire at the point of my departure I would reflect on this ineffable love. I would speak to those around me and share with them the marvel of the evidences of His love in my soul. 'Tis greatly wise to talk with our last hours', wrote a poet of old, and this I would truly wish to do. I am always quickened in my soul when I talk of Himself. Surely it must have the like effect when on my dying bed? In writing this I take into account the possibility that I may not have the faculty of speech or the energy to make myself heard. But dying can not silence until He wills. Would it not be indeed precious to work for Him, even when feebleness and a lisping tongue is our lot? Speaking of Jacob's death, Spurgeon says "He was immortal till his work was done. As long as God had another sentence to speak through him death could not paralyse his tongue".

I had a most unusual experience some months ago. I was in the monthly prayer meeting when suddenly, while the congregation were singing verses in Psalm forty six, in Gaelic, I felt as if I were hearing the refrain in the distance. For a few seconds it was as if I was on my death bed and these verses were being sung to me. So strong was the illusion that when the sensation wore off I desired that they would indeed be sung in these circumstances by the same presenter, singing the same tune. I have never quite understood the experience although at the time I did interpret it as my forthcoming death. The words were these:

'A river is whose streams do glad
The City of our God;
The Holy place, wherein the Lord
Most high hath His abode.

God in the midst of her doth dwell;
Nothing shall her remove;
The Lord to her an helper will,
And that right early prove.'

But my journeying thoughts have not just led me to dwell on the process of dying, the Jordan of Death, the Glories of Glory or the deathbed of departed saints. No, I have also dwelt on the mundane, the possible need for medication, the arrangements for my funeral and the hope that I may die in my own home and be buried from there, despite an absence of close relatives. Surely, if Jacob before gathering up his feet into bed and yielding up the ghost, gave command in relation to his burial, 'bury me with my fathers', and Joseph, on advising his brethren of his imminent death, extracted from them a promise that they would take his bones up with then whem they left Egypt, it is right that I should record my wishes in this respect.

On my discharge from hospital two years ago my mind became pre-occupied with the administration of drugs as these might affect myself. I now share my silent musings, which remained with me with such clarity and conviction that I wrote them down, simply because of the meditative channels into which they led me. They must not be taken out of context and they are not recorded as worthy of consideration. They are merely the product of mental activity, meaningful only to myself. They should not be regarded as an ideal to be achieved, or a goal to be attained, or an example to be followed. There is no ideal but the way of the Cross. Each person is led so differently, so individually, yet, so wondrously. There is no goal but Jesus, the author and finisher of our faith. It is His race we run and we must run it according to the dictates of His will. There is no example but that which He has left with us.

8th May 1992

'Awake for quite a while in the early hours of the morning. for some reason my thoughts found recourse to the drug regime instituted for the relief of pain in the terminal phase of some cancers.

'I know not what my Lord has in store for me but I do know that whatever it may be it will be absolutely right. The God, from whom the substance, of my yet imperfect being, was not hid when I was made in secret, must surely be well acquainted with the great and final summons of my life. Of course He is. I have nothing to fear because He ordereth aright and He will do so in the administration of any treatment I may yet require.

'As I write I reflect on the grace of the person who on being asked what his choice would be, a sudden or a lingering death bed, responded, "It would be my choice to have no choice at all". What wisdom! Choice bound up in His Will. While I endorse this, I find myself with very definite views on medication for the relief of pain in my own case. Perhaps the reason for my own contrary views and feelings will only be clear on my death bed.

'It is my wish that if drugs are required, these will only be administered after consultation with me, after my views are known and the drug of choice has been discussed. If my condition is too low then I would wish to be allowed to die quietly unless I give a sign that I am in need of something to ease pain. I do not wish to receive anything simply because it is assumed I require it. Is this going too far? Maybe, but it is what I genuinely want and I hope that when the time comes, if it does, my wishes will be honoured.

'Pain is experienced by all creatures from birth. Like death it is the result of sin. Pain may be simple or quite troublesome, yet, we seem to live in reasonable acceptance of it. Why, when life is about to expire, is it decided that, irrespective of tolerance, pain should be irradicated from our experience because this is what we are bound to expect? "How can we deliver good pain control?" is a question the professions often ask themselves, but I have never heard it asked. "Does the patient want pain control if the pain is within her threshold?" This is what I personally want. How can Christians understand some of the references to pain in scripture if drugs expunge it from their consciousness? I am not talking here of intractable pain. Common sense tells that this requires appropriate analgesia. I am talking of what may be bearable for me and making a plea, that my views of what is acceptable to me will be acceptable to those caring for me.

'When I consider the positive things which are told about Heaven, one is that, 'there will be no pain there'. Surely this reflects an expectation that pain will be in our experience here and that it will, at some time, be of reasonable intensity. How otherwise could we appreciate its absence, as Scripture outlines? But why should I feel as I do about this forerunner? For no other reason, I hope, than that I may enjoy the company of the Lord's people for as long as I humanly can without my reactions being dulled or my judgement impaired. I want to be sure that what I say on a spiritual level is thought through rationally and not drug induced - Lord, preserve me, if it be Thy Divine Will, from drug induced euphoria; may what I seek be solely for Thy Glory and the advancement of Thy Kingdom. Lord, activate the thoughts of my earthly physician so that these desires may be bound up in the unity of Thy purpose. Thou art the Great Physician. Thou knowest my case better than any. Didst Thou not ordain it? Dost Thou not know what I can endure and what I can not and what Thou wilt help me to bear? Dost Thou not know how best I can serve Thee until my final breath is drawn? Yes, Sovereign Lord.

'To enjoy the fellowship of the Lord and His people is supreme, even when I ponder the weak debilitating state of my mortal frame as it descends into the Valley. I come back to this, I would not like my concentration dulled or my mind fuzzed by the effect of drugs until thinking and conversation are an effort and sleep my only desire. I make allowance for my actual needs at the time. It would be wonderful Lord, to be conscious of Thy presence, to be able to commune with Thee, to give expression to Thy dealings with my soul and to make some positive contribution towards the fellowship of Thy children, whom I hope and pray will call to see me and gather around me as I make the solitary descent. I hope, however low my condition, that Thy dear children will not feel they ought not to hold fellowship with one another and with Thee, except in quietude. I wish them to behave as if I were fully conscious of their presence and part of their company, which I will be whether my condition permits them to acknowledge this or not. I hope they will pray audibly, read the word audibly and sing the precious psalms with joyful voice, expressing themselves, if that is their wish, in the words of the Psalmist:

> 'Then filled with laughter was our mouth
> Our tongue with melody.'

'Yes, heavenly melody and heavenly laughter around my death bed is the desire of my heart, in the hope that God's Kingdom will be furthered and Satan's receive a crushing blow.

'Whatever happens to me I would like to go out from this world with His praise on my lips and His love in my heart, extolling His Wonders to poor, sinful, desperately wicked me. I would like to comprehend what is happening around me and to absorb His read word and that to His honour. For all of these reasons I would be unhappy, if I did require drugs, if these were administered too early - Lord of my soul, Keeper of my life, control this aspect of my care. But not my will but Thine be done. Sanctify me Lord by the process through which I must go and help me, above all else, to be in absolute agreement with Thy purpose for my life, whatever that may be. Thy plan is infinitely greater than anything I could ask. Thy care transcends human knowledge, every hair is numbered and not even the sparrow falls to the ground without Thy knowledge. This is too wonderful. Who but infinite God could care thus!

'Thy knowledge is too great for me
Too high to understand'.

'Amazing knowledge, amazing care. Who could not fully, implicitly and with patience commit themselves to One so attentive of every detail of our lives and our death and our dying. One so profound in Wisdom, so unchangeable in His Being, so Holy we cannot countenance Him, whose goodness exceeds our comprehension and whose essence is very truth - Lord Jesus, mould me, fashion me, fit me to be Thy vessel. Open my mind to grasp what Thou art so patient to teach and attune my will until it is in complete harmony with Thine own.

'Let me prevail with Thee Lord, until, like Jacob, I too may in wrestling call out, 'I will not let Thee go except Thou bless me'. Oh! for that constraining spirit '.... abide .... for it is toward evening and the day is far spent'. Lord, tarry with me now and forever more. Help me to keep my face Zionward, in the strength of the blessed word and in the full knowledge that, as with all the other walls which confronted me, Thou wilt assist me in overleaping those which I may yet encounter.'

Very recently I came across an account of Halyburton's death bed which Spurgeon has prefaced thus, 'It has been sometimes said that death bed excitements are produced by delirium or caused by drugs, yet there are multitudes of clear cases where men have had no delirium and have been altogether untouched by drugs as is the case of Halyburton, who said, "My bones are riving through my skin and yet all my bones are praising Him; I have peace in the midst of pain and how much I have experienced of that! Strange that this body is going away to corruption and yet my intellect is so lively that I can say there is not the least alteration, the least decay of judgement or memory".

When I wrote my thoughts that morning in May 1992, I had not stepped into the presence, figuratively speaking, of any of the dying saints I bring before readers in this chapter. I hope I will be forgiven for suggesting that if their minds had been under the influence of analgesia we may not have had those blessed expressions on record, some surviving, as in the case of Jeremiah Whitaker, four hundred years. "All is of mercy this side of hell", he said to his friends. "Oh! my God", he went on, "break open the prison door and set my poor captive soul free; but enable me to wait willingly Thy time. I desire to be dissolved. Never was man more desirous of life than I am of death. When will that time come, when I shall neither sin nor sorrow any more". As his dissolution drew nearer his pain became more acute, but the Grace of God supported him and so wonderfully succoured him that his faith and patience never abated.

Richard Baxter, on his death bed, taking hold of something when his pain was at its zenith, used to say, "Press on Richard to the Saints Everlasting Rest". Beautiful words, which are now quite famous. Thankfully, today there is remedy for acute pain, we do have medication, but there was no medication in this era. These men required to be totally dependent upon and specially sustained by their God.

'Lord I am pained, but I resign
To Thy superior will
T'is Grace, T'is wisdom all divine
Appoints the pain I feel'

Moody Stewart (1898) wrote of joy abounding by suffering. "For weeks I had been suffering and for a time I thought the discomfort had left me, but it returned more sharply. I prayed for sleep but was not satisfied it was the Lord's Will to grant it. I had that evening been much helped in asking a full gift of the Holy Spirit. After lying down, the distress became such that nothing could counteract it except the joy of the Holy Ghost and this was granted to me in such abundance, yet without the slightest alleviation of my suffering. The joy was so great I could rejoice in the pain with no desire for its removal ....". Who can understand this? None but those to whom the experience and the grace is given.

Few are able to write of the triumphant condition of their mind, as Dr. Payson did in his dying hours. "If I were to adopt the language of Bunyan I should date this letter from the Land of Beulah of which for some weeks I have been a happy inhabitant. The Celestial City is in full view. Its glories beam upon me, its odour wafts to me, its sound strikes into my heart. Nothing separates but the river of death which now appears an insignificant rill that may be crossed in one step whenever God gives permission. The Son of Righteousness has gradually been drawing nearer and now fills the whole hemisphere pouring forth a flood of Glory in which I seem to float as an insect in the beams of the sun. Exultant yet trembling I gaze into His excessive brightness and wonder ... that God should deign thus to shine on a sinful worm. A single heart and a single tongue together inadequate. I want a whole heart and a whole tongue to express that emotion". What ecstasy! What an exalted state of faith and feeling. 'If this be dying', said another, 'It is worth living for the mere sake of dying'. Dr. Payson could certainly say that.

I share these death bed scenes to encourage my own soul and the souls of others, who may be approaching the bank of the river and who may be fearful and despondent at what lies ahead.

Christian, as we saw earlier, was indeed fearful but when Christ met his soul with his truth the enemy was as still as a stone and when he and Hopeful reached the other side of the river they were met by two Shining Men who said to them, 'We are ministering Spirits, sent forth to minister to those that shall be heirs of salvation', and accompanying them, as they walked towards the gate of the Celestial City, they spoke of the glories thereof.

> 'Scarce had earth and all its glitter
> From my fading vision fled,
> When at once came forth to meet me,
> Christ, my ever blessed head,
> And before His gracious presence,
> All my terror sped away,
> All the clouds and mist and darkness,
> That had e'er obscured my day'.

While I still live down here on earth it would be wonderful to live submissive to His Will, doing what is His pleasure. McCheyne used to say 'Live so as to be missed'. And those who countenanced his death, at the age of twenty nine years, did not doubt that he had lived his life by that which he recommended to others. As the summers of my own life become fewer my thoughts frequently turn to my terminal phase and my constant prayer is, that He will prepare me and fit me for this final part of the journey, that His grace will be sufficient for me and that His strength will be made perfect in my weakness. Yes, the sun will surely set and I may not be able to describe what it will be like or to exclaim as Janeway did, "Oh! that I had lips to tell you a thousandth part of that which I now feel". God knows how I will be ushered out of this world and into the next. It sufficeth that He does. It is possible that my cancer may not be the means God ultimately uses to take me to Glory, but over the years this has come to be my expectation. I have thought of the vital organs in my body which may yet be affected by cancer and of the debilitating state into which this could physically bring me. Inasmuch as it is possible to live into any unknown circumstance I have done that. The thought that I may depart this life by any other means disappoints a little. I hasten to add, not for the same reason as my aunt expressed disappointment. Mine is earthly, hers belonged to His Glory. By whatever means He takes me it will be gloriously right.

When we consider the chariot by which God has uplifted so many of His children from this earth, it is an elevated position for a disease so dreaded by so many. God uses only that which is best for us. If cancer is the disease by which, under His Divine Control, my soul is ultimately transported I would like it to be thought of in a positive light. What He uses to accomplish His Will can only be 'very good'. So shall it be with us. Former things are going to pass away. When, at death, the shell of the believer's cancer is finally cracked it will hold only honey. Out of the carcase of Samson's lion came sweetness, the sweetness of honey. It is sweetness that awaits us in the land which floweth with milk and honey.

It is told that Queen Victoria's daughter, the Princess Alice, abundantly testified to the Christian character of the departed in the simple consolation she offered to one of her tutors who had lost a daughter. "There is but one who can give you consolation", she wrote, "The souls of believers are at their death made perfect in holiness and do immediately pass into Glory - Yes, immediately. There is to the departed spirit no middle state between earth and heaven. Swift as never light went, swift as never thought went, flies the just man's spirit to Glory. One moment the sick room, the scaffold, the stake, then the great deep swell of the angel's song".

'But ye are come unto Mount Sion, and unto the City of the living God, The heavenly Jerusalem and to an innumerable company of Angels.'